"THE WEIGHT WE CARRY

A BLUEPRINT FOR DEALING WITH LIFE'S BURDENS"

"THE WEIGHT WE CARRY"

Polokwane, South Africa

Copyright © 2023 by Moses Moreroa

All rights reserved. No part of this book may be reproduced, stored in a retrieval system, or transmitted, in any form or by any means, electronic, mechanical, photocopying, recording, or otherwise, without the prior written permission of the copyright owner, except in the case of brief quotations embodied in critical reviews and certain other non-commercial uses permitted by copyright law.

This book is a work of the author's opinion, experiences and research. The information provided in this book is for general informational purposes only and is not intended as a substitute for professional advice. The author and publisher assume no responsibility for errors or omissions, or for any damages resulting from the use of the information contained herein.

Any resemblance to real persons, living or dead, or actual events is purely coincidental. For permission requests, write to the publisher, addressed "Attention: Permissions Coordinator," at the address below:

Information Giants Publishers™
1256 Waterfall Business Park
Midrand, Gauteng Province, 2195
South Africa

Website: www.informationgiants.co.za
Email: info@informationgiants.co.za

ISBN: 978-0-7961-1558-4

Cover Design: Information Giants (Pty) Ltd

Printed and bound in South Africa

First Edition: August 2023

For enquiries or bulk purchases, please contact:

Moses Moreroa
PO Box 54
Haenertsburg, 0730
South Africa

Disclaimer: The information and advice provided in this book are not intended as a substitute for professional counselling, therapy, or medical advice. Readers are advised to seek the guidance of qualified professionals regarding their specific situation or circumstances.

The names of specific companies, products, or individuals mentioned in this book are provided for illustrative purposes only and do not constitute an endorsement or recommendation unless otherwise indicated.

Your support of the author's work is appreciated. Thank you for respecting the hard work of the author and the rights of the copyright holder.

"THE WEIGHT WE CARRY"

A BLUEPRINT FOR DEALING WITH LIFE'S BURDENS

Table of Contents

Letter to Self i
Acknowledgment v
Preface vii
Mental health - whose problem? xi
Chapter One 1
    Clean Your Mind 1
Chapter Two 19
    An Unprepared Generation? 19
Chapter Three 40
    Winning In The Backyard 40
Chapter Four 49
    The Power of Anticipation 49
Chapter Five 60
    Be Your Chief Executive - Visionary 60
Chapter Six 74
    Let Go of Validation Seeking 74
Chapter Seven 82
    Mastering the Basics of Life 82
Chapter Eight 97
    The Placebo Effect 97
Chapter Nine 104

Illusion of Control	104
Chapter Ten	**109**
How You Live Is What You Leave	109
Chapter Eleven	**112**
Self-Hate	112
Chapter Twelve	**117**
Sometimes It's Not About You	117
Chapter Thirteen	**129**
It Begins With You	129
Chapter Fourteen	**145**
Emotional Hygiene	145
Chapter Fifteen	**148**
We Often Regret Not Doing	148
Chapter Sixteen	**156**
Pressures of Life	156
Chapter Seventeen	**169**
Distracted & Destroyed	169
Chapter Eighteen	**175**
Solute or Solvent Friends?	175
Chapter Nineteen	**181**
Activity Without Productivity	181
Chapter Twenty	**182**
Hasta La Vista	182

Chapter Twenty-One 184
    Afraid Of Being Afraid 184
Chapter Twenty-Two 186
    Close The Cracks 186
Chapter Twenty-Three 189
    Sowing Discord In Fields Of Peace 189
Chapter Twenty-Four 192
    Strength In Stillness 192
Chapter Twenty-Five 195
    Pearls Before Swine 195
Chapter Twenty-Six 198
    Not Immediately But Definitely 198
Chapter Twenty-Seven 199
    To Survive Or To Thrive? 199
Chapter Twenty-Eight 201
    Still, Black Tax 201
Chapter Twenty-Nine 204
    Still, Pride Goes Before Destruction 204
Chapter Thirty 205
    Loose Lips Sink Ships 205
Chapter Thirty-One 207
    To Rob Peter To Pay Paul 207
Chapter Thirty-Two 211

Be My Guest 211

Chapter Thirty-Three 212

Sankofa 212

Chapter Thirty-Four 215

A Paycheck Away From Poverty 215

Chapter Thirty-Five 217

The Fire-Fighting Approach 217

Chapter Thirty-Six 220

When An Adult Doesn't Want To Mature 220

Chapter Thirty-Seven 222

The Looking Self Glass 222

Chapter Thirty-Eight 229

Jump Before You're Pushed 229

Chapter Thirty-Nine 232

Feather Dusters Were Once Peacocks 232

Chapter Forty 234

Unlike Charges 234

Chapter Forty-One 236

The Dangers of The Beginning and End 236

Chapter Forty-Two 242

Cracks Success Will Never Fill 242

Chapter Forty-Three 245

The Law of Energy 245

Chapter Forty-Four 249
   The Art of Sorry 249

Chapter Forty-Five 250
   Resource Vs Source 250

Chapter Forty-Six 255
   Dare To Use It 255

Chapter Forty-Seven 259
   Conspicuous Flexing 259

Chapter Forty-Eight 262
   Life Balance Sheet 262

Chapter Forty-Nine 266
   Body, Mind and Money 266

Chapter Fifty 270
   Epilogue 270

Bibliography 273

Index 278

The Weight We Carry: A Blueprint for Dealing with Life's Burdens

Letter to Self

Private Bag X2023
Inner Me
Comfort Zone
0000

Private Bag X2024
Introspection
Mental Health
0000

RE: Just checking in

Dear Self,

How are you holding up, my beautiful mess? I can't help but wonder: why do I bother asking when it's clear that life has thrown you into a whirlwind?

They say mirrors reflect what stands before them, yet there's so much more to you than meets the eye. Why doesn't the mirror show the battles you fight within?

Under the surface, you're desperate and shattered, but all the mirror reveals is the outward beauty gracing your face. Deep down, you tremble and break.

Why do you continue to support those who disregard your struggles? Look at yourself, my dear self. Why do you passionately help them face their own demons while, in your time of need, you're left alone without their aid?

Self, I've heard you whisper those words, "Enough is enough," but you keep giving more than you should. You're fully aware when they exploit you for their selfish gain, yet you remain entangled. You've gone above and beyond your comfort zone to ensure their well-being, but deep down, you and they both know they're taking advantage.

You know very well that being with those friends compromises your true self, yet you strive so hard to fit in. You spend beyond your means to impress people you hardly know, even though deep down you question the purpose.

Self, here's the truth: you yearn to look good in the eyes of those who don't truly care. Yet you neglect those who have always been by your side—the ones who notice when you're not yourself, when the weight of the world bears down on you, when your burdens become too heavy to carry.

Self, the moment you started competing with those who never dreamed of reaching your level, you allowed vulnerability to seep in. You publicly criticise what you privately adore. Is it because you feel insecure, anxious, and uncertain? Your day begins with thoughts of how others can be wrong, making it difficult to embrace hope, love, and care.

Self, you rarely praise and often condemn. You even go to great lengths to sabotage yourself, hoping to make others appear worse off than you. Why are you so harsh on yourself? Surely, it can't be pleasant to dislike everything you see.

Honestly, the more you prioritise others in your life, the more they learn to prioritise themselves over you. Promoting others over yourself only teaches them that you can be relegated to a secondary role.

The Weight We Carry: A Blueprint for Dealing with Life's Burdens

Why do you always complain about bad friends? Let me share a secret with you: not everyone in your life is meant to be for you. Don't hold acquaintances too close to your heart; they're merely present due to circumstances. Circumstances are transient, and they will eventually move on. Learn to collaborate with people rather than serve them. Otherwise, you'll find yourself with no meaningful purpose, as your worth, importance, and relevance revolve around people who come and go.

Self, please remember that sometimes it's not about you. You may do everything right and still face the worst outcomes. Your best efforts may be average for someone else. You won't find peace of mind if you constantly prioritise others over your own needs. People who disregard your feelings will always place you at the bottom of their priority list. They won't consider you when they act. Loving yourself means breaking the cycle of excessive expectations from others. Being content with who you are means understanding that love alone isn't enough if it's not reciprocated.

Sincerely,

Myself

Moses Moreroa

For the wanderers exploring the vastness of their potential, may this book be your compass in the unknown.

The Weight We Carry: A Blueprint for Dealing with Life's Burdens

Acknowledgment

Writing this self-help book, "The Weight We Carry," has been a transformative journey that I could never have embarked upon alone. Throughout this process, I have been fortunate to receive guidance, support and inspiration from numerous individuals who have played a significant role in bringing this book to life. Their steadfast belief in the importance of self-discovery and personal growth has been both humbling and motivating.

First and foremost, I would like to express my heartfelt gratitude to my family, whose love and encouragement have been my foundation. To my mother, Putla 'Nogane', who instilled in me the values of perseverance and curiosity, I owe a debt of gratitude that words cannot adequately express. Thank you for always being my pillar of strength, even when the path was uncertain.

I must extend my sincere appreciation to my friends and colleagues who served as beta readers and provided constructive feedback on early drafts. Your candid remarks and keen observations have played a crucial role in refining the content of this book and ensuring its accessibility to a wide audience.

To the countless individuals whose stories and experiences have contributed to the embroidery of this book, thank you for bravely sharing your struggles, triumphs and personal growth journeys.

I must also recognise the support of the publishing team—Information Giants Publishers™, whose dedication and hard work have been instrumental in bringing this project to fruition.

Lastly, to the readers of "The Weight We Carry," thank you for choosing this book as your companion on your path to self-discovery. My deepest hope is that the ideas and exercises within these pages will empower you to embrace your true self, find your true north, unlock your potential, and cultivate a life filled with purpose and fulfillment.

Remember, this is a journey—a journey to become the best version of yourself. As you embark on this voyage of self-discovery, know that you are not alone. May you find strength, clarity, and joy as you delve into the depths of your being and harness the power within.

With immense gratitude,

Moses Moreroa

The Weight We Carry: A Blueprint for Dealing with Life's Burdens

Preface

Imagine a school of thought, hidden and overlooked, but truly genuine. You won't find it through a search engine because it was just my train of thought. So, there's no need to venture further. Just keep reading, and let me share my revelations about mental health.

Being correct is not merely regurgitating information or recalling things as expected. It's about understanding the right way to approach things. Allow me to illustrate my point using a classroom scenario. When a math question is given to a student to solve, the teacher often refers to the answer key or a memorandum to assess the student's work.

Let's consider a question like this:

4 + 2 - 3

= 3

Now, imagine if the student arrives at a different answer, such as:

2 + 2 + 1 - 1

= 4

According to the answer key, the student's response would be marked as wrong because it was not what was asked. But here's my question: Is the student truly wrong? The calculations were correct, and the answer was consistent.

If I were the teacher, I would consider it a correct solution because the calculations were accurate, regardless of the unconventional method. We often judge things as wrong simply because we have a set of answers before asking the question.

The same principle applies to mental health. We tend to be excessively critical of ourselves based on external circumstances rather than the reality of our inner selves. In the classroom example, the purpose of the test was not to assess how the student would perform in that specific situation (the exam), applying knowledge and thought process, but rather to evaluate their understanding of calculations. Similarly, in life, we sometimes become depressed over setbacks that do not define our entire being or determine our future.

We may fail at one thing and allow it to overshadow everything else. Maybe we didn't secure employment while our peers did, or we couldn't buy a car when a friend did. Perhaps our life milestones don't align with those around us, such as marriage or income levels.

Here's the crux of the matter: temporary versus eternal. There's a vast difference between the two, and how we perceive this difference greatly impacts our sense of peace and contentment. If we focus predominantly on the temporary aspects of life, we struggle to find contentment and often find it difficult to cope. However, if we shift our focus to the eternal (the future), a tremendous burden can be lifted from our shoulders. Finding peace in the eternal requires effort. It's easy to allow the temporary aspects of life, the day-to-day struggles, to consume all our energy and attention. Our jobs demand our utmost focus (temporary), our physical bodies require constant maintenance (temporary), and the state of our finances can mercilessly sway our emotions (temporary). We may feel elated when we have plenty of money and despondent when we don't.

The Weight We Carry: A Blueprint for Dealing with Life's Burdens

Keeping up with material possessions becomes an all-consuming task. If we let it, the temporary, physical aspect of life can become a harsh taskmaster.

If only we understood that temporary situations can derail our grand plans but are not a sentence to failure, we would realise that we are on the right track. An educator, unrestricted by temporary situations, would not penalise a brilliant student who struggled in a momentary test but inherently understood the essence of the subject matter.

Now, zoom out and look at the bigger picture. A lack of mental health is never a consequence of permanent situations but temporary obstacles. People often expect everything to go perfectly in the present and fail to see the grand tapestry of life. As 2 Corinthians 4:18 beautifully states, *"So we fix our eyes not on what is seen, but on what is unseen since what is seen is temporary, but what is unseen is eternal."* While this biblical quote doesn't directly underscore my point, it guides me down the path that there's more to life beyond the fleeting moments. If we were to live solely for the present, we would have no future to look forward to.

Moses Moreroa

Self,
Others
and Building Up

The Weight We Carry: A Blueprint for Dealing with Life's Burdens

Mental health - whose problem?

When we feel better, we do better.

Mental health affects everything. It affects our nature and how we interact with the world and ourselves. *Show me one person who is free from mental malaise.* I have had a few engagements with mental health activists and, to some extent, the nurses and practitioners treating it, and to date I do not know what mental health means or is. To put it pedestrianly, mental health affects how we think, feel and act. But I am more fretful and frantic to imagine how our thinking, feelings and actions affect the state of our being. We treat mental health as if it's more of a result of what happens to us extrinsically (what comes to us) than what we do to ourselves (between ourselves).

Without good mental health, we are susceptible to not knowing our full worth and struggling with things that are beyond our control. When we ignore mental health, we ignore ourselves.

We must value our health and wellness as much as we value anything else, if not more. We must learn that we are good enough, that we are worthy of compassion, and that others are too.

This leads us to have higher standards. It helps us feel sad if we want to feel sad, accepting our state of mind. And it also helps us do something about it.

We don't have to wait to feel better; we can feel better today simply by acknowledging our struggles as real and worth paying compassionate attention to.

We don't need to solve every problem, but we can ask for help if things get too much—I mean, more problematic. Then, and only then, do we gain some sense of control over our lives again.

The biggest mistake in life is thinking that we are born normal and innocent. Hold on, I am not ascending the spiritual realm. Spare me the creation framework.

The notion that we are born into this world as inherently normal and innocent can be one of the most significant misconceptions we encounter in life. Now, before you assume I'm delving into the realms of spirituality or espousing a creationist framework, let me clarify.

From the moment we enter this world, we bring with us a complex tapestry of *genetics, experiences* and *predispositions*. None of us are born as blank slates or devoid of influence. We are shaped by the interplay of nature and nurture, a unique combination that forms the foundation of our being.

It is crucial to acknowledge that our individual journeys begin with inherent complexities. Each of us carries a unique set of strengths, weaknesses and predispositions. While innocence may be attributed to the lack of conscious wrongdoing, it does not negate the fact that we arrive in this world with inherent intricacies that shape our path.

Recognising this truth allows us to embrace our authentic selves fully. It frees us from the burden of unrealistic expectations or the pursuit of an illusory state of normalcy. Instead, we can acknowledge and appreciate the beauty of our individuality, understanding that it is through our complexities that we find our true essence.

The Weight We Carry: A Blueprint for Dealing with Life's Burdens

We all deserve to have peace of mind. Mental health is important because we deserve it. If we only knew how worthwhile we were, we could take over the world. It's our own limiting thoughts that hold us back, as we think that we are not normal, broken or not worthwhile.

The truth is that the mind can lie. It can hold us back. And yet it is also the source of everything good we experience.

It doesn't make anyone less of a person to experience mental health issues. When we value mental health, we lead better lives. It doesn't mean everything will be better overnight, but we can learn how to value ourselves so we can improve over time.

Our mental health affects how we cope with life. Lack of treatment leads to hopelessness and sadness, worthlessness, feeling guilty, anxiety and worry, fear, and loss of control.

Our relationships may suffer. Our performance in any situation, such as school or work, may decline. Withdrawal and isolation may happen.

Indeed, when our mental health suffers, various aspects of our lives may be impacted. We may lose interest in activities we once enjoyed, leading to a decline in our overall motivation. Our ability to manage tasks and time effectively may deteriorate, causing disruptions and disorganisation in our daily lives. Concentration becomes challenging, and we may find ourselves caught in a cycle of rumination or fixating on cleaning and organising as a means of coping.

Our relationship with food can also undergo significant changes. We may experience fluctuations in appetite or engage in disordered eating patterns. Racing thoughts may become more prevalent, making it difficult to find inner calm and clarity. Life, as a whole, can feel overwhelming, as if everything is spinning out of control.

In severe cases of mental health issues, individuals may begin to lose touch with reality, experiencing hallucinations or hearing voices that are not there. Self-harming behaviours may emerge as a desperate attempt to cope with emotional pain. Destructive patterns, such as excessive alcohol or drug use, may take hold, exacerbating the existing mental health challenges. Regrettably, in the most distressing circumstances, suicidal ideations may become a haunting presence.

It is crucial to take mental health seriously and seek appropriate support and treatment. By doing so, we can address these symptoms and regain stability in our lives. Professional help, therapy, medication, and a strong support system can provide the necessary tools and guidance to navigate these difficult times.

Remember, neglecting mental health can have far-reaching consequences, leading to a cascade of detrimental effects across various areas of our lives. Taking proactive steps to prioritise mental well-being is essential for maintaining balance, resilience and overall quality of life.

Mental health encompasses various dimensions of our well-being, including our *emotional, psychological* and *social* aspects. It significantly influences how we handle stress, establish relationships with others, and make decisions. Mental health is relevant and important throughout all stages of life, from childhood to adulthood.

The Weight We Carry: A Blueprint for Dealing with Life's Burdens

The development of mental health problems can impact our thinking, mood and behaviour. Multiple factors contribute to the emergence of these issues, including biological factors like *genetics* or *brain chemistry*, *life experiences* such as trauma or abuse, and a family history of mental health problems.

In understanding mental health, it is recognised that behaviour is not solely a result of conscious thought processes. It is also influenced by automatic functions and processes that lie beyond our conscious control. This perspective highlights the complexity of our psychological makeup and the interconnectedness of various factors that contribute to our mental health.

Within the field of psychology, different schools of thought and approaches exist, leading to variations in treatment methods for mental health conditions. There is no one-size-fits-all approach, and interventions may vary based on individual needs and preferences and the specific nature of the condition being addressed.

Ultimately, the goal of mental health care and treatment is to facilitate a process of personal transformation and growth. Recovery involves changing attitudes, values, feelings, goals, skills, and roles in a deeply personal and unique manner. It is about living a fulfilling and hopeful life, even while acknowledging the limitations caused by the illness. Through this journey, individuals can discover new meanings and purposes, allowing them to contribute meaningfully to their own lives and the world around them.

Cognitive Behavioural Therapy (CBT) is a therapeutic approach that has been developed within the mental health model of addiction. In the context of addiction treatment, CBT is used to help individuals identify the cognitive processes that contribute to relapse and work towards modifying these thoughts and behaviours to avoid risky situations (American Psychological Association, 2020).

In a drug rehab programme based on the mental health model, various elements are incorporated to address a patient's psychological well-being and resolve underlying issues.

For example, therapy sessions may focus on unblocking emotions that are tied to childhood trauma, providing a safe space for individuals to explore and process these experiences. Additionally, therapy may involve helping patients understand and address resentments they may hold and guiding them towards appropriate ways of confronting the individuals involved. Sometimes, simply providing individuals with an opportunity to express their emotions and allowing them to cry can be a cathartic and healing experience (American Psychological Association, 2012).

These interventions aim to delve into the psychological aspects of addiction and address the underlying factors that contribute to substance misuse. By exploring and working through these psychological elements, individuals in addiction treatment can gain a deeper understanding of themselves, develop healthier coping mechanisms, and ultimately reduce the risk of relapse.

It is important to note that the mental health model recognises the complex interplay between psychological processes, individual experiences, and addiction. By incorporating therapeutic approaches like CBT into addiction treatment programmes, individuals are provided with tools and strategies to enhance their mental well-being, promote long-term recovery, and improve their overall quality of life.

Chapter One

Clean Your Mind

There was a farmer who lost a precious watch in his barn. This watch held immense sentimental value for him, so he embarked on a thorough search to find it. Despite his best efforts, the watch remained elusive among the haystacks. In a stroke of inspiration, the farmer sought the assistance of a group of children who happened to be playing outside the barn. He promised them a reward for whoever could locate the watch. Excited by the prospect of a prize, the children eagerly joined the search.

They scoured every nook and cranny, carefully combing through the hay, but to no avail. Just as the farmer was losing hope, a little boy approached him and asked for another chance. Intrigued by the boy's determination, the farmer agreed and sent him back into the barn. After a while, the little boy emerged with the watch in his hand. The farmer was overjoyed and amazed, curious to know how the boy had succeeded where others had failed. With a smile, the boy explained his method.

He said, "I did nothing but sit quietly on the ground and listen. In the stillness, I could hear the faint ticking of the watch, guiding me towards its location."

The farmer was struck by the simplicity and wisdom of the boy's approach. He realised the power of a peaceful mind and how it can enhance our thinking and perception. The boy's ability to tune in to the silence allowed him to focus and make a sharp observation that led to success.

From this encounter, the farmer learned an invaluable lesson. He understood that a calm and peaceful mind has the capacity to think more clearly and make better decisions. When our minds are cluttered and agitated, we are prone to making rash choices, engaging in thoughtless reactions, and succumbing to anger.

To harness the power of a peaceful mind, the farmer resolved to incorporate a few minutes of silence into his daily routine. He discovered that these moments of stillness helped him to align his thoughts, set his intentions, and navigate life with greater clarity and purpose.

In this tale, we learn the importance of cultivating a peaceful mind. By allowing ourselves moments of silence and stillness, we can enhance our emotional intelligence, make wiser choices, and lead a more fulfilling life aligned with our true desires.

> *Researchers estimate you have about 60 000 thoughts each day. And many of those thoughts involve thinking the same things over and over again.*
>
> www.inc.com

The Weight We Carry: A Blueprint for Dealing with Life's Burdens

Rehashing the same things, *focusing on the negative*, and worrying about things you can't control wastes your time and *your mental energy*. The key to building more mental muscle involves *decluttering* your mind of those mental habits that are keeping you stuck.

Three tips that will help you spring clean your brain and rid yourself of the thinking patterns that keep you from reaching your greatest potential.

1. Get rid of the pity parties

It is essential to recognise the distinction between experiencing healthy sadness or disappointment and indulging in self-pity. While feeling sad or disappointed is a natural and necessary part of the human experience, self-pity involves dwelling on our misfortunes and convincing ourselves that our problems are insurmountable and worse than those of others. If we allow self-pity to consume us, it can keep us trapped in a cycle of negativity and hinder our progress.

True happiness doesn't hinge on external factors such as relationships, vacations, jobs, or wealth. It begins within our own minds and the thoughts we consistently tell ourselves. The stories we internalise and the narratives we create shape our perception of the world and influence our overall well-being.

When we catch ourselves hosting a pity party, it is crucial to make a conscious commitment to take positive action. Even if we cannot solve a particular problem, such as a loved one's health issue, we can still choose to do something meaningful to improve our own lives or contribute to the well-being of others. It could be as simple as practising gratitude, engaging in acts of kindness, or pursuing personal growth and self-care activities.

By redirecting our focus towards positive actions, we break free from the grip of self-pity and empower ourselves to make a difference, no matter how small. Taking proactive steps, even in challenging circumstances, allows us to regain a sense of control and resilience, propelling us forward on our journey towards personal growth and contentment.

Decluttering tip: It's crucial to be vigilant for language that perpetuates a victim mindset. Phrases like "No one understands" or "Bad things always happen to me" can be indicators that we are filling our minds with unhelpful and negative thoughts. Recognising these red flags is the first step towards breaking free from a victim mentality.
When we catch ourselves thinking in this way, it's important to pause, take a deep breath, and consciously shift our focus.

2. Challenge your self-doubt

Self-doubt is deeply ingrained and cannot be overcome with empty affirmations. Merely telling yourself you're amazing won't drown out negativity. To tackle self-doubt effectively, confront negative thoughts directly. Prove to your mind that you are capable and competent. Each time you challenge your self-doubt and demonstrate your abilities, your perception of yourself will gradually shift. Consistent effort in challenging self-doubt will reshape your thinking patterns.

Decluttering tip: *You need courage, not confidence*, to take action. When your mind questions your capabilities, respond with a resolute "*Challenge accepted*." Embrace the opportunity to prove your doubts wrong and recognise that your mind isn't always accurate in its assessments.

3. Distinguish worrying and ruminating from problem-solving

Whether you're struggling to pay your bills or you're having a hard time dealing with a co-worker, active problem-solving is helpful. *Rehashing the same things over and over, imagining catastrophic outcomes, and second-guessing your decisions won't get you anywhere.*

> Mentally strong people exist. But they are not a miracle. They do not have special insensitivity powers. Or easy lives. Or big budgets. Or extra time. They do not confuse being mentally strong with acting tough.

Decluttering tip: Schedule 15 minutes every day to worry and ruminate. When you catch yourself thinking about something outside those 15 minutes, remind yourself that it's not time to worry yet. Then, when you reach the scheduled worry time, sit down and worry. Then, you'll confine your worries to one small chunk of time rather than allowing them to take over your entire day.

I once found my niece crying so painfully, with a lake of tears severely streaming down her face. I asked what was wrong, and she told me that her friends bullied her at school. When I asked for their reasons, she said they were mostly jealous of her success in

> The mind of a mechanic works from a broken point of view.

the classroom. They said she was sleeping with teachers to get good grades. I asked her, "Do they take anything from you by talking badly behind your back? For you to move to the next level, do you need their validation? To know and appreciate the truth and to take lies to the mind, which one comes with peace of mind?" Without thinking twice, she replied and said, "But uncle, I no longer have peace. I don't even want to go to school anymore. I am beginning to lose confidence. I even deliberately wrote wrong answers in my last test to at least get an average mark." I asked if the bullying had died down after she lowered her standards. Sadly, it never stopped.

They then said she did not open her legs; that's why the latest script came out exactly how it should have been all along. This is what happens when we listen to people more than we listen to ourselves. We live in a world where people want to see you do good, but not better than them. If you don't approve of your talents, you will allow germs to enter your mind. The negative thoughts of others come as microorganisms to us; we have to clean our minds in order to stay healthy.

I like how car mechanics work; when you take your car to his workshop, even if it's brand new, he will look for faults. His job is to find faults. He will not be satisfied that the car does not show any signs of fault. The mechanic can even break certain things while trying so hard to find something wrong.
The mind of a mechanic works from a broken point of view. If nothing is broken, they don't have a life.

I advised my niece to simply refrain from dwelling in a mental space where she becomes vulnerable to negative thoughts and bullying. Instead of allowing haters to hinder her progress, she should focus on her strengths and talents. The way you structure your mind, your beliefs, and how you present yourself daily determines your overall well-being.
It is crucial to cleanse your mind and eliminate anything that taints it. Think positively, feel refreshed, and live a happy life.

Our daily lives can be likened to a computer's desktop interface. The appearance and organisation of the desktop reflect the user's preferences and desired control. If the desktop is cluttered, it doesn't imply a problem with the computer itself; rather, it is the user's doing. If the screen strains the eyes, it suggests incorrect display settings or excessively high brightness levels.

Similarly, our minds are programmed to function like a desktop interface. Each day, we encounter numerous choices from the moment we wake up, just like opening our computers. In a world of abundant choices, being organised is of utmost importance. Have you ever noticed that when your morning starts in chaos—hitting the snooze button, skipping breakfast, and rushing out the door—the rest of your day tends to reflect that disorderly mood? You may find yourself easily offended, even when no offence is intended. How you plan your day profoundly affects your emotions, actions, and thoughts throughout the day. Additionally, how you perceive negativity from others also influences the outcome of your day.

Don't believe me? Try leaving your house for work or your room for classes without properly grooming yourself. Your thoughts will likely convince you that everyone knows you didn't take a thorough shower. When someone rubs their eyes, you might start to imagine crusty rheum on your own eye corners. If someone sneezes, you may conclude that there's an unpleasant odour emanating from your mouth or underarms. It all originates in the mind. Therefore, it is essential to cleanse and organise your mind, treating it as you would a desktop interface.

The size of your icons

Like when the user of a computer has the option to determine the size of icons on the desktop through the view option on the dropdown menu as you press a right click. Your everyday life is exactly how you prefer it. You'd either view the files as small icons, medium icons, large icons, auto-arrange icons, align them to the grid, or show or hide them.

Your mind is like a desktop. Even in your life, your feelings are the sum total of how you decide to view things that happen to you. In the midst of being bullied, my niece decided to see it as something too big. She set her icons to large view. It could have been a small issue if she programmed her mind in such a way that it didn't matter if she was bullied because it wouldn't change the fact that she was brilliant. How you prefer to understand the behaviour of others in your space, be it at school, work, or a social gathering, changes the outlook of your day. My niece took her clean mind from a state of perfection to a state of weakness, where the opinions of her haters mattered more than her reality. She took her well-functioning car to a mechanic.

Another case may be on your way to work; someone you know might pass you by without greeting. You can either ignore the thought that he or she hates or is jealous of you. Like how you'd decide to show or hide items to appear on your desktop, or make it a small issue that won't really change the outlook of your day.
When you think too hard about it, you start to create scenarios that do not even exist. You think they're angry because you bought a new fridge that has a water dispenser. Only to find out that they've not seen it being delivered. You assume they're jealous because your son-in-law brought groceries, only to realise they only came home late in the evening yesterday. You heard sounds on your roof and concluded that they tried to bewitch you, and now they're bitter because they

The Weight We Carry: A Blueprint for Dealing with Life's Burdens

could not get to you. Your day is surely going to be spoiled. You will spend it thinking about the things you shouldn't have.

Choose the right view. Like you would on your desktop. Be in the right frame of mind. Be positive about your life. When others regret loving a cheating partner, embrace the one you managed to love. When others feel like they should be somewhere in life, appreciate that wherever you are, you're preparing. When others feel bad about their past, don't blame yourself for who you should have become by now; you can only work today for a better tomorrow. Don't spend your capital to keep up with someone who is spending their profit. Don't fake it until you make it; face it until you make it. Whatever you do, no matter if it's good or bad, becomes part of your personality. Do it for you more than someone else. Make it work for you. Prepare your mind for optimal productivity without attaching 'what ifs' and other negative influencers. You can't have large icons on your desktop if the view is not pleasant. Change the settings. Change your mind. You can't have too many files on the desktop, it will affect the view of the background picture. Remove unwanted files and organise others in folders to avoid leaving them scattered on the desktop. Cleanse your mind.

These are things that happen to you when you set your viewpoint incorrectly. Don't make issues out of nothing; they only affect you more than the next person. It ruins your day, not those you view negatively. It disturbs your peace of mind, and the people you're worried about don't even know that you're worried. Don't set large icons on your desktop if you're going to struggle with working on them. Equally, don't set the size of your icons to medium or small if it will bother you. Either way, you're in control. Do what will work for the betterment of your goals. Cleanse your mind. Occupy your mind with the right viewpoint. Ease your nerves. Align your goals for the day the same way you'd align icons on the desktop. If icons are scattered, it becomes difficult to locate the right file. Do not just wish for your day to go well, prepare for it. Set objectives and timelines. Give yourself enough time to finish. Don't fall for the temptation that things will fall into place once you start working. The desktop will never be aligned if the user leaves it cluttered. A student who often understands the notes better has organised them before the lecture. He or she even marks the areas to focus on. Nothing will work itself out in your day until you align your goals with the vision you have for that day.

Sort your icons

Again, you can sort your desktop icons by name, size, item type, or date modified. This helps you know where to look when you want to locate or open a file. A student who highlights his or her notes knows when to begin reading after taking a few hours break or the next day. Just like an administrator or receptionist puts files in alphabetical order.
Imagine going into a surgery with a migraine and the receptionist taking longer to pull out your file.

The same way a stock packer won't put a large tin of fish in front of the medium or small size on the shelf or put cleaning items in a row where there's food stuff, items in a supermarket are sorted according to types: food, cosmetics, etc., and even when a building of a mall is planned, the planner creates a food court, bank section, kids' corner, clothes area, supermarkets, furniture stores, hardware stores, etc., and the shopper knows which direction to take when looking for certain items.

Some people are overwhelmed by almost everything in one day. They start so many tasks and fail to finish any of them. Like the desktop, you can put as many files on it as you possibly can. It will even have some in the screen margins. It never gets full as long as the memory is available. It fills the space. Like your mind, it is an untamed ocean of thoughts and feelings, pulsating as if waves are crashing against the inside of your skull. When you don't sort your mind and channel it, determining what to have and what to disregard, it will be a matter of time before your head disappears below the surface of the water, like files that are on the desktop but below others since there's no more space.

Sorting your icons is like setting priorities to avoid being under pressure. If your goal is to study, your friend wouldn't convince you to go shopping. This is like the background picture or wallpaper on your desktop. If you choose to put on animations or fleeting wallpapers, you're more likely to be distracted while working.

Set up your desktop the way you'd work effectively. If your mind isn't in the right state, you don't have a clear vision. It takes time to find yourself. Cleanse your mind. If the desktop is too bright, reduce the brightness before it blinds you. Control the colours. Choose the right theme, because that's what you will see every time you unlock the laptop. So, don't let others choices undermine yours because you will be unhappy every time you wake up. Choose which notifications should pop up on your task bar or desktop every time you're connected to the Internet. Configure your mind properly.

Don't stop and check everything that passes by or comes into your life; focus on what you're doing for the day, like others are doing with their lives. The journey isn't perfect, but the purpose is. Never doubt your plans. Don't harbour any negativity. Do away with anything that tells you that "you can't do this." Doubt your doubts before you can doubt your faith.

Send what's not needed to the bin

Interestingly, every desktop is configured with a recycle bin. Which means it is given the function of clearing the unwanted items on it. Even in your mind, there's a function for deleting everything that's not needed.

Do not keep toxic items on your mind. Keep your mind fresh and clean. You have the ability to send to the trash anything that no longer has a place in your life. When the desktop is full, the user of the computer sees it. There's no excuse why it shouldn't be clean.
When you get to the depression stage, you know you've been holding onto things you're supposed to delete. You keep checking your ex-lover's profiles every day, which clutters your mind.

The Weight We Carry: A Blueprint for Dealing with Life's Burdens

Remove that file and create a clean desktop. The friends you keep are a representation of who you are. *Remove* any friends who don't help you do better. Keep the files you need on the desktop. That is, surround yourself with people who are meaningful to your purpose. *Remove* friends who don't understand your vision and aren't going to contribute to your to-do list. Your worry is misleading you; *remove* it. If your partner treats you wrong, they're not going to change; *remove* them from your life. Removing things that are not needed from the desktop is a powerful way to make your working space clean and balanced.

Cleanse your mind, too. Letting go of things that no longer serve any purpose in your life gives your mind clarity, focus, peace, and stability. We are demotivated to do better in life because we clutter our minds with unnecessary, energy-draining negativity. Rid of those things. Stop holding on to useless things. The truth is, unless you let go, unless you forgive yourself, unless you forgive the situation, and unless you realise that the situation is over, you can't move forward. Forget what hurt you, but never forget what it taught you. For a bird to fly high in the sky, it has to leave the ground.

You, too, take off from the ground of doubt, fear, lack, and demoralisation. In the process of letting go, you will lose many things, but you will have space for greater things.

Small changes can create huge opportunities in your life. Dispose of these things every day, thinking there's a perfect time. Don't back away when you start to get nervous about your dreams. Don't wait until you're no longer afraid; it may never happen. Send that doubt to the bin—*delete*. Stop listening to the negative voice inside. There's no extra special person; successful people have learned not to listen to dream killers. Many people get a strange sort of satisfaction in telling others that things won't work—*delete*!

The recycle bin has various options: open, empty, and rename. Although you've tried to clean your desktop, when you open the recycle bin, you will find everything as good as it was on the desktop. The very same unnecessary items are still on your desktop, but grouped together. This is when you let go but fail to forget. You keep opening the recycle bin to remind yourself of what you had. And once you open, there's an option to restore.

Be careful not to open files you've deleted; all will be restored to their original state. Don't feel bad about removing certain people from your life. Don't mind being ridiculed. Don't care about the naysayers. Don't let the critics get to you again. Empty your bin to have a healthy lifestyle. If the garbage remains in the bin for too long, your health will be at risk.

Empty your bin. Rename and redefine what occupies your mind. When you clean up your life, you create a new sense of purpose, drive, and commitment. *When your file says written fear, replace it with I'm determined.* Rename. *If your gut tells you that you won't make it, tell it that you're more certain than ever.* Rename. *If people tell you that you're a mess, say it's a message.*

Rename. Tell them that you're trusting the process of building, and any construction site may be a mess, but that does not define the house. If they think you have little to make an impact, tell them you will produce the best with what you have and maximise your minimum, like David did when he took on Goliath. Clean your mind and live a shameless life. Cleanse your mind and create space for limitless possibilities. For your puzzle-building to make sense, you have to start on a clean slate. Only throw the right pieces into your space. Have the bigger picture. Then begin building. Small things matter. Never underestimate the power of tiny things that look insignificant. Many strong relationships were destroyed by a piece of an earring. A small dent on the shirt. A two-minute phone call. The best lessons we learn in life are the ones we learn over and over again. The human mind needs lots of reminders—and lots of practice—to operate effectively.

For example, deep down, we know it's OK to…

> Say "no"
> Speak up
> Tell the truth
> Believe differently
> Change our mind
> Prioritize our needs
> Learn from our mistakes
> Embrace our imperfections
> Forgive and seek forgiveness
> Begin again, stronger than before

Yet, we often seek the exact opposite when life gets stressful and we're under pressure.

We do the wrong things even when we know better. The human mind, like any other muscle in the body, has weaknesses. It can become forgetful and less responsive when under stress. However, these weaknesses can be conquered through regular practice.

The mind is like a muscle, and it, like any other muscle in the human body, requires exercise to gain and maintain strength. It must be trained daily to grow and develop gradually over time. If you have not pushed the mind in a variety of small, positive ways over time, it will crumble on the inevitable days when things become overwhelmingly stressful.

If you are determined to cleanse your mind, repeat this affirmation, which I believe will motivate you to keep going:

> I will produce the best with what I have. I will maximise my minimum. I will endure the pain for my gain. My life's downs will be the source of my many crowns. Such tests will be testimony once I'm done. I've messed up, but this is tomorrow's message. I will listen to the tiny voice that says, 'You can try again tomorrow.' And I won't quit; I was born a genius, and I am wired for success. I won't hesitate. I will act on my dreams. I will choose the right view and sort my files into order according to size, date, and type. I will understand that my background is my motivation to do well. I will delete and remove any unnecessary files from my system in order to maintain a clean mind. I won't let anyone or anything define me. I will rename anything that defines me from without. I am prepared to empty my bin.

Chapter Two

An Unprepared Generation?

Nowadays, there is a concerning increase in depression among young teens and adults. It seems that, despite having access to life's luxuries, we inadvertently invite the pressures of life. The South African Depression and Anxiety Group (SADAG) has reported alarming statistics, with the country experiencing approximately 23 suicides and 20 attempted suicides every day. In under a year, SADAG has received around 55,000 calls for help. There are various factors, both obvious and deeply ingrained, that contribute to suicide, such as relationship issues, work stress, unemployment, trauma, grief, and financial difficulties. Unfortunately, many individuals lack proper access to mental health treatment and care. Additionally, people often struggle to know where to seek help, and the stigma surrounding mental health prevents them from speaking up until it is too late. SADAG has noted that the majority of callers seeking assistance are women, including those reaching out on behalf of their loved ones, as South African men commit suicide at a rate five times higher than women. While the statistics are significant, it is crucial to understand the underlying causes rather than solely reporting on the unfortunate numbers. It is essential to address these issues and work towards prevention.

Bottom line, we all want fulfilment and success; this is the end of our mental health. Most people don't start the day off saying, "Well, today I'm going to try to feel like an empty failure." So often, though, we can get into a rut of self-degradation and complacency when it comes to our daily lives. It is because we want to have what we can't have and neglect doing what we have to do.

When graduates leave a university or college, even matriculants begin to confront the reality that everything there has been built from scratch. Nothing is for taking. So, these age groups compete, mostly between themselves, and do as others do or don't do as others don't.

THE UNEMPLOYED PRESSURES:
The Molotov cocktail

The first three to four years at university are exciting but also the hardest and most challenging. At this point, students begin to make choices that will usher them into a life they have always imagined while under the care of their parents. One studying media hopes to be a mogul, if not a successful personality. The other person in management wants to open a business and lead a successful empire. You can add to the list; it is endless. Almost all industries are oversupplied with graduates.

Let's look at the pressures that come with unemployment while your classmates, friends, relatives, and enemies are getting ahead. You die every second when you think about it, and social media inflates the whole lot. This group thinks they are invincible, so when they feel psychological pain, they are more likely to feel overwhelmed by hopelessness and the belief that they have no control over their lives. Having to ask for money to make copies, sending lots of applications

with regret messages, and not affording sanitary pads and other toiletries as a woman is breaking.
The strong ones resort to survival of the fittest antics, like women prostituting and trapping men with babies to secure relationships while men steal or take drugs.

However, those who do not have the courage to traverse the tunnel of despair, desolation, and dreadfulness experience what we call the *Molotov cocktail* that triggers teen suicide.

Molotov cocktail

A Molotov cocktail is a type of projectile weapon also known as a petrol bomb, gasoline bomb, bottle bomb, poor man's grenade, or Molly. It consists of a glass bottle filled with a flammable liquid such as petrol, alcohol, or a napalm-like mixture, as well as some motor oil. A cloth wick is secured to the top of the bottle with its stopper and is usually doused in alcohol or kerosene. When used, the wick is lit and the Molotov cocktail is thrown towards its target. When it smashes the burst of fuel is ignited, creating a fireball. Sometimes toxic substances such as bleach or acids are added to the cocktail, turning it into a makeshift chemical weapon.

The Molotov cocktail got its name from the Winter War between Finland and the Soviet Union in 1939. Finns used it in reference to Vyacheslav Molotov, the Soviet foreign minister at the time. He was key to the Molotov-Ribbentrop Pact with Nazi Germany, which defined the borders of Soviet and German influence across Finland, Poland, Lithuania, Latvia, and Estonia.

Like a mixture of flammables in a bottle, the youth concern themselves with a life from without. They want to spend the money they don't have to please people they don't know.

They internalise so many toxicities to the extent that they believe their own lies. These acts vary mainly according to gender stereotypes. But the effect is the same: wishing for the life of someone who is 50 when one is just 20.

For ladies, looking rich is fundamental to securing a front seat on social media and at occasions such as lifestyle centres. Many have a number of frontal wigs of late, from polyurMotumee to mesh, combo, and open weft units. These come in the longest inches you can ever think of. You find someone who holds a degree or just a matric and is not working, investing in hair, not necessarily to look good for themselves but to make friends envy them and imaginary 'haters' die of jealousy. They tend to conceal less and reveal more. There's nothing wrong, by the way.

If we were to look at the root cause, you would realise that a third of seven- to 10-year-old girls believe that they are judged on their appearance, and a quarter feel the need to be perfect. Girls suffer from a crisis of body confidence and feel under pressure to be pretty. As they walk the streets, boys usually pay attention to those they deem beautiful and ignore those who, to them, are not. That is why girls would group themselves in those categories. The most beautiful flock together, or otherwise. Society therefore makes young girls believe and feel that their looks are their most important attribute. When boys call a girl and she doesn't give them attention, she is then called ugly. They knew this would go to her heart and pierce her. Why? Why is education not thrown in as an attribute? Why are girls judged more on appearance than ability? This girl would feel embarrassed by how she looked. Girls grow up seeing physical appearance as the most important area of investment in their lives. This is serious. As a society, we need to face the fact that objectification and harassment are ruining girls' lives, and we are letting it happen. *This is the first flammable they add to their Molotov cocktail.*

This feeling is exacerbated among graduates who believe they need to attract the finest of associations, such as men and fellow ladies. They go to the extent of fishing men, who seem to be well off. This is to secure the finer things in life, like going to hotels for content on their Instagram pages. They target driving guys for road trips and adventure content. Remember what Sean Covey said: *"We become what we repeatedly do."*

> *"Sow a thought, and you reap an act; Sow an act, and you reap a habit; Sow a habit, and you reap a character; Sow a character, and you reap a destiny."*
>
>   Samuel Smiles, Happy Homes and the Hearts That Make Them

It is a pity that before they know it, they have lost a sense of self. Some go to the extent of going into clothing stores to fit the most expensive and stylish wear, taking photographs, and pretending it is theirs. Some raise money mysteriously to buy designer clothes, whereas others rent them. They go out every weekend "*beke le beke*" and proudly call themselves "*ba strata*." They say with trends like "every little money I get, *na* enjoyment," what one would call a movement of instant gratification. After what they call a dope or massive weekend, they get back to their reality of lack.

For gents, they suffer the same stressors. To look good and be seen to have money so they can lure the ladies who look sophisticated and "sexy". What would one call a contest of deceit? *This is the second flammable they add to their Molotov cocktail.*

The activities done at the whereabouts include heavy drinking, unplanned sexual, mostly unprotected, intercourse. Smoking weed, which I don't know how they normalised. These nightlife activities come with health complications from taking drugs and unprotected sex. *This is the third flammable they add to their Molotov cocktail.*

That is why, these days, it is rare to find a lady and a gentleman in their early twenties without a child who live in extreme poverty. Most of the children are born out of entertainment rather than a mutual relationship. The gentlemen abandon them. That is why you find a mother with three kids with different fathers. A man has three kids with different mothers. When they reach a point of wanting to settle in life, they have so many maintenance orders that they become stepparents at a younger age. This brings unprecedented dynamics to relationships and leads to physical and emotional abuse, constant differences, poor planning, and cheating. This, in some way, exacerbates gender-based abuse in one form or another. It is not easy to leave such relationships because the partners have pretended to be formidable forces in public and cannot bear the shame of separation. I will not dwell much on this; you get my point. *This is the fourth flammable they add to their Molotov cocktail.*

It really worries me. We go about our daily routines with a heavy load on our minds. It might have to do with losing weight, getting older, being lonely, family dilemmas, stagnant career progression, debt problems, or any one of a myriad of other troubles that land in our "deal with this challenge" inbox. Yet, despite all this stuff that exists below the surface, when someone says, "How are you?" we are most likely to say, "I'm fine!" Now, I get that it would be odd if we went around complaining and wallowing in self-pity all day long. Who would want to be around that?

But there is going to be a downside to all this suppression, denial, and other defence mechanisms that we all employ to help us cope with our daily lives.

In simple terms, not seeking recourse adds to our daily frustrations. *I know there are campaigns that encourage people to speak up, but society has not been taught how to respond when someone speaks up.* Some say there are two options in life: you open up and become a meme, or you bottle up and become a memory. Most people who speak up get even more victimisation and are shamed. There have not been highly effective therapy systems in society. But this is a topic for another day. The point I want to drive home is that we bottle so much at an early age, and in no way advice works because we live more of a deceitful life than our reality. *This is the fifth flammable they add to their Molotov cocktail.*

We do our best to avoid dealing with the discomfort that is a natural part of being human. We use avoidant coping to deal with challenges in life. Long-term denial can lead to self-sabotage and an inability to know what is real and what is fabricated. We justify all sorts of things to ourselves in order to live a life as free of internal conflict as possible (see my blog post on cognitive dissonance).

Sure, we can try to dismiss our thoughts and be more aware when we are using cognitive distortions such as catastrophising, negative filters, personalising, or black-and-white thinking in order to minimise the emotional impact of too much pretending, but I have witnessed, over and over again, clients trying too hard to explain away life challenges that cannot effectively be explained away.

That is why, when it all boils down to a point of return, when one cannot pretend anymore and cannot live their reality, ending their lives becomes the most viable solution.

That is when the Molotov cocktail is now thrown into the deep end, and it shall explode. We harbour too many flammables inside.

This, unfortunately, does not start at an advanced stage of life. It rears its ugly head in school with little, innocent things like casual Fridays. It exposes the inequality among the children. It goes on to manifest in high school at the adolescent stage. Being two-faced and appeasing the company you are with is what many kids do in order to be popular. Fit in, don't be different, and definitely don't be yourself—these are messages that modern school dynamics unwittingly teach. Schools are like acting academies. You learn to do what you must to not be bullied, to not stand out, and to be popular. It's just "not in" to tell others you don't like something that goes against the consensus. And so the conditioning begins. In short, too much pretending is inadvertently encouraged in school. I will not labour on this point; it needs its own discussion.

These flammables that we bottle inside are fuelled by a street culture of fitting in and appearing to be relevant. Here is how we mostly make cardinal mistakes by taking bad decisions that at first do not really look like mistakes but are what we "ought" to do to survive.

Masking Poverty

The Weight We Carry: A Blueprint for Dealing with Life's Burdens

Poverty extends beyond mere financial circumstances or income measures. It encompasses a state of mind, generating feelings of anxiety and shaping both society's perception of individuals and their own self-perception. Consequently, people living in poverty encounter numerous limitations that exceed their economic resources. They endure heightened stress levels and face social pressures that exacerbate their challenges.

Regrettably, there are those who perceive individuals in poverty as lazy and treat them as inferior, perpetuating negative stereotypes. In response, people living in poverty often feel compelled to hide their economic situation to seek fair treatment and avoid judgement.

While taking one of my random village drives sometime in 2017, what struck me more than the poor infrastructure in so many villages was the residents' pride. Young women walked by with brand-name purses and deep green jade bracelets, while men drove home to their shabby shacks with shiny cars and dope rims. Had I seen them in the downtown business district, I would have believed they belonged there.

Limpopo's urban society, Africa's actually, is in fact one of the most consumerist and superficial in the world—I mean, my world or the world I have travelled. I have seen more people showing off iPhones here than I have anywhere in Europe. But it makes you wonder: if a family has three generations of family members sleeping in one room together, why do they choose to spend their money on big TVs or going to nightlife clubs? In the words of Harvard professor Mullainathan, "You and I can be busy, and we take a vacation from work. You can't take a break from being poor. You can't say, 'Hey, I've had enough of worrying about money; I'm just going to be rich for a couple of weeks until I've recovered'." Vexed by financial worries and trying to avoid humiliation by their society, poor people might sometimes make financial decisions that don't make sense at first glance. But if buying a big TV is just the thing that will help distract them from their troubles, they should be able to spend their money as they like.

In South Africa, however, this masking of poverty has taken on new dimensions, particularly because of the judgmental nature of its urban

> Perhaps if the elite stops judging the impoverished of society by their own standard, and tries to empathise with the psychological effects of financial pressure and uncertainty, they can better understand the financial decisions of the poor.

elite society.

Young girls from rural families (as well as upper-class South African women) cover themselves in whitening cream with the idea that looking more white makes them look less 'peasantlike' and thus more wealthy or at least nourished. Is it because the West calls them people of colour? Many women do this to get accepted at well-paying jobs, while others do it to get attention and be liked. People from rural areas living in the city are often looked down upon and disrespected, so they try to hide their background under expensive-looking clothes.

Even the poorest apartment block will only parade expensive German cars in its parking lot, if any at all. While in South Wales, my neighbour at an apartment I stayed in was a beautiful Chinese woman. We once

The Weight We Carry: A Blueprint for Dealing with Life's Burdens

travelled together from South Wales to Cardiff. On the way, she was highly concerned about her face and kept applying some powder. When I asked if everything was okay, she said she didn't want to look shiny. She told me about what she said was the Chinese principle of *mianzi* ("face"), which dictates that an individual must retain respect from others and never be humiliated. But most of all, it has to do with the fact that poor people want to finally be taken seriously by the elite.

South Africa is riddled by youth unemployment, but the outlook on the street contradicts the facts. For instance, the poorest of the poor in South Africa still consider it a status symbol to be a mall goer, but even those who can't afford anything in the mall go just to enjoy the glamorous surroundings and free air conditioning. Of late, young men who are barely working class—they are just having a job—go to make seemingly reasonable purchases of shiny cars and luxuries on the basis of microcredit, which actually traps them in debt and high interest rates for years to come. Debt is the biggest enemy of the impoverished, yet the social pressure to appear wealthy often forces people to ignore this.

Simultaneously, the media and citizens of developed nations are so accustomed to the helpless, lazy "slumdog" that they don't deem him capable of being anything else and become judgmental when he spends money on a luxury rather than food.

Society and poor people themselves might realise that their lifestyles are actually more resourceful, that they do not often waste money on things that they don't need, and that they have deep bonds with their family and neighbours that enrich their lives. Without experiencing so much external pressure to save face, poor people might be able to regain their self-respect and pursue more sustainable methods of evading poverty.

It is not surprising that most people in need learn the science of making bad decisions for tomorrow in order to save face today.

> *I am convinced that our greatest fear is not poverty, but rather being harshly judged for being poor.*

The science of making bad decisions

There's no denying that we all make bad decisions from time to time. But why does it seem like certain people make more bad decisions than others?

Like vs. Lust

Scientifically and psychologically speaking, there are two kinds of pleasure to which our brains respond: "liking" and "wanting." The pleasure known as "liking" is a state of happiness and satisfaction, such as the gratification we get after a good meal. But the pleasure known as "wanting" is a little different. This comes from the pleasure of pursuing something and feeling seduction or excitement.

The Weight We Carry: A Blueprint for Dealing with Life's Burdens

Basically, it's the lust and thrill of the chase, such as going after that "bad boy" in high school or university or seeking out hit after hit of that drug of choice, alcohol, hubbly bubbly, etc. Research has revealed that dopamine, a neurotransmitter in the brain, plays a significant role in generating the sensation of wanting, reinforcing our brain's desire for more. So, we'll stop at nothing to get what we want—even if we know we'll regret our decisions later. But being mindful of this compulsive way of thinking can help, enabling us to play the tape all the way before taking action. There is your open secret; what you do about it, I don't know.

Not having something makes us want it more

Another factor that plays into bad decision-making is that we human beings naturally want what we can't have.
When we are told that we can't have something, our brains want it more. This manifests even in toddlers. When I was in high school, for example, I used to fantasise about fashion and mostly expensive stuff because I came from one of the poorest families in my village. Being raised by a single mother and now making it to university, it was something I needed to prove that I was now a better person. But at the time, university was even more expensive. I stayed on campus, and that increased my student debt. The NSFAS, which was a loan by then, could not cover my tuition costs, and I did not get the Wizit card (later renamed Fundi). I was poorer. But I could not look poor in my village; I had to save face. A whole university student? Don't get me wrong, I've always liked the finer things in life, but being told

I couldn't have most of them for a number of years sent my obsession through the roof!

The same goes for anything else, which could be dieting, smoking, or drug use. Suddenly depriving yourself of everything might make those cravings even more powerful, so it's best to give into "rare indulgences" from time to time, such as a bowl of ice cream or a drag from a cigarette. But from a drug addiction standpoint, a slip-up or two could have much more damaging effects. Instead of focusing on the fact that you can't have something, it's better to learn to reframe ways of thinking and choose to fill that space with new people and outside interests. There you have it—an open secret.

To save face, what I did was take my last R800 and buy what looked like a beautiful Samsung S3 smartphone. At the time, it was the "in thing". That month, I did not have groceries and leeched on unsuspecting friends.
I would later, precisely two weeks later, discover that it was not a smartphone but a demo phone. It couldn't take quality pictures anymore, apps stopped working, and the internet browser disappeared. *That was my first scientific mistake—faking it, hoping to make it—and I was hard done by. The open secret is that you will not get everything in life, and it might just cost you more than it would if you forced things.*

"What the Hell" Effect

This basically means that once we've misstepped, we use it as justification to go all out. Think, "Well, I've already spent this guy's money and had sex with him before, so, what the hell, I might as well have unprotected sex with him." Basically, in this scenario, our one bad decision can snowball into bigger consequences, making us temporarily lose sight of ourselves, our values, and our vision. We stop caring about the next day because we have already committed the first mistake we thought we would avoid today. Dubbed the what-the-hell-effect or counter-regulatory behaviour by dieting researchers Janet Polivy and C. Peter Herman, the phenomenon describes a cycle of indulgence, regret, or shame, more indulgence, more regret, or shame, and so on. At the end of the day, we are "wanting" creatures. Everything we do is connected to our wants. Sometimes we want things even when we don't want to want them. Understanding the centrality of wants—or goals, expectations, dreams, values, yearnings, ambitions, intentions, hankerings, objectives, targets, hopes, aims, longings, attitudes, proclivities, missions, standards, motives, purposes, plans, specifications, benchmarks, aspirations, desires, needs, passions, inclinations, wishes, and cravings—will help you get more of what you want, or strive for, more often. It will also help you understand those times when you might be perplexed because you did something you were sure you didn't want to do.

An important thing to appreciate about wants is that they are all about results, not actions. So, if you want to understand (there's another want) why you acted in a particular way, think about the result, not the behaviour. Sometimes it's even hard to describe what we want or why we acted in a particular way, but the existence of a want doesn't depend on our ability to describe it or talk about it. People have wants before they learn to talk. Even if you can't put into words why you did something, it's still the case that there's a team of people all busily going about the business of achieving the results they're required to produce.

So if you ever have the experience of seemingly doing something you don't want to do, think about the result of your action. Sometimes it can take a bit of meandering through the back streets of your mind, but you'll know it when you find it.

> All I can explain this feeling is that we often want what we don't want to want.

The Weight We Carry: A Blueprint for Dealing with Life's Burdens

Can we ever prepare youth?

In my master's research, I conducted a study on leadership and the necessary skills for the future. The data collection phase of the research spanned across five countries, including both Nordic countries and countries in the Global South. The aim was to explore the evolving nature of work and its impact on individuals.

The findings of the study indicated that 15-year-olds today can anticipate having more than 17 jobs in various industries throughout their working lives. This highlights the significant changes and transitions that individuals will likely experience in their careers.

> So, what do you want to be when you grow up?

However, the research also shed light on a concern: many young individuals may not be adequately prepared to navigate this dynamic work landscape. Why not?

We have been asking this question of children and young people since the start of the Industrial Revolution. Whatever answer young people proffered—engineer, accountant, hairdresser, dentist, teacher, scientist, doctor—would then point them to the training they would need and whether they should go to university, TVET, or enter an apprenticeship.

Today, that question no longer serves. The assumption on which it is predicated—a single career for life in a stable workforce—is now false.

The world of work is in massive transition to an ever more global, technology-driven, flexible economy in which whole professions are being altered, new professions are coming into existence, and traditional jobs are being swallowed by automation.

To cite just one example, app developers were a rare breed until the launch of the iPhone in 2007; now it is a thriving industry in its own right—at least for now, until a new technology comes along and apps face their own Kodak moment.

The research further looked at how leaders confront exciting change and help their subordinates earn their daily bread. The theme sought to understand the dimensions of this change, the implications for young people—and thereby, the future of every country—and what we need to do to prepare young people for their economic lives. A leader who leads uninspired and debt-ridden employees has more to do than translate the company's vision.

The study I conducted focused on three key economic forces—automation, globalisation and collaboration—and their impact on the future of work. The research concluded that in a constantly changing world, today's 15-year-olds can expect to have more than 17 jobs in five different industries throughout their working lives.

One aspect of my research was to assess how well young Australians are being prepared for this future reality. It became evident that young people will need a range of essential enterprise skills to thrive in an evolving economy. These skills include digital literacy, critical thinking, creativity, financial acumen, flexibility, collaboration, and self-sufficiency.

However, the findings indicated that many young individuals are not adequately equipped with these necessary skills. Data revealed that a significant portion of South African 15-year-olds lack proficiency in financial literacy, problem-solving, and digital literacy. Furthermore, with the changing landscape of work, more young people will need to become job creators rather than rely solely on traditional job-seeking roles. Unfortunately, there is limited emphasis on embedding enterprise skills within our education systems.

To further highlight the importance of these skills, I compared the skills sought by employers just a few years ago to those currently in demand. The analysis of job advertisements for positions requiring less than five years of experience revealed a remarkable shift. The demand for digital skills has increased by over 200 percent since 2013, including critical thinking by over 150 percent, creativity by over 60 percent, and presentation skills by 25 percent. These skills are now considered fundamental prerequisites for entering the workforce and will be even more essential in the future.

The study also emphasised that jobs traditionally associated with technical skills, such as dentistry, environmental engineering, and veterinary science, now require a strong emphasis on digital literacy.

It is clear that the preparation of youth for the future of work must begin early. Action is needed urgently, starting with an investment in an enterprise education strategy. We should teach enterprise skills in primary school and build upon them year by year throughout high school. It is crucial to deliver these skills in ways that resonate with students, incorporating experiential learning and peer engagement. By taking proactive measures, we can equip the younger generation with the necessary skills and competencies to navigate the future world of work successfully.

To prepare for the fluid, complex, and enterprising new work order, it is crucial to provide support to teachers so they can effectively equip students with the necessary skills. Additionally, parents should be informed about the skills their children will require to navigate multiple careers successfully. Engaging students, schools, industry stakeholders, and parents is essential in fostering an understanding of the changing work landscape, which, although less stable and predictable, offers abundant opportunities.

To achieve a future-ready workforce, we must embed the new basics into the core of future generations' education. By investing in and inspiring the next generation, we can equip them for a radically different future of work, ensuring Australia's future prosperity.

When engaging in conversations about the future with children and young people, instead of asking the traditional question, "What do you want to be when you grow up?" we should encourage them to consider the kind of opportunities they want to create. By reframing the conversation in this way, we not only encourage young individuals to think beyond predefined career paths but also foster their preparedness to seize opportunities as they arise.

Currently, we are witnessing a mismatch between youth who are ready but not prepared and those who are prepared but not ready for the changing work landscape. This mismatch often leads to a sense of misfit and can hinder their ability to navigate the evolving job market effectively. Addressing this disparity requires a concerted effort to bridge the gap between readiness and preparedness, ensuring that young individuals are both equipped with the necessary skills and ready to seize opportunities that come their way.

> We are currently experiencing a crisis of youth who are ready but not prepared, and those who are prepared but not ready.

Chapter Three

Winning In The Backyard

Young people are facing the most significant disruption in the world of work since the industrial revolution. When writing this section, one thing that kept me in the loop was the philosophy of football teams and how they make or break records.

In team sports, the term home advantage, also called home ground, home field, home-field advantage, home court, home-court advantage, defender's advantage, or home-ice advantage, describes the benefit that the home team is said to gain over the visiting team. This benefit has been attributed to the psychological effects supporting fans have on the competitors or referees; to the psychological or physiological advantages of playing near home in familiar situations; to the disadvantages away teams suffer from changing time zones or climates or from the rigours of travel; and in some sports, to specific rules that favour the home team directly or indirectly.

Hence, the away goal rule, also known as the away goals rule, was introduced in many tournaments as a method used to determine the winner of a two-legged tie when the aggregate score is tied after both legs.

It is primarily used in the knockout stages of tournaments, such as the CAF Champions League, UEFA Champions League, and UEFA Europa League. The significance of the away goal rule is to provide an additional factor that can influence the outcome of a tie, giving an advantage to the team that scores more goals away from their home stadium. The rule was introduced to encourage more attacking play in away matches and add a strategic element to the competition.

Under the away goal rule, if the aggregate score (the total goals scored by each team over the two legs) is tied, the team that has scored more goals away from home is declared the winner. In other words, away goals count as more valuable than home goals when determining the winner.

The rationale behind this rule is to reward teams that perform well in an away match, as it is generally considered more challenging to score goals in an opponent's stadium. The rule also aims to prevent teams from playing defensively in away matches and relying solely on home advantage in the return leg.

Most coaches would be fired for losing home games. It is assumed that the pressure is less at home. Could it be that the reason Amazon is so big is that when Jeff Bezos created Amazon in his garage, he had more time to perfect his craft without pressure?

Apple's founders, Steve Jobs, Steve Wozniak and Ronald Wayne, developed the first Apple computer in 1976 in the garage of 21-year-old Steve Jobs' parents' house. Jobs and Wozniak wanted to make computers small enough for people to have in their homes or offices. Apple is now the most successful international tech giant in the world.

Although Steve Wozniak did clarify that their garage was not the birthplace of their designs, he says that the *garage was something for us to feel was our home. We had no money. You have to work out of your home when you have no money."*

Okay, I think I am taking it too far. With winning in your backyard, I mean being full of positive thoughts and affirmations about your life. Your backyard is your mind; that is your humble beginning. In your mind, no one knows how hard it is to face each day but you. In a mansion, no one knows about the days the occupants went to bed without a decent meal.

All of life's greatest things originate with an assortment of humble beginnings. Although minuscule and seemingly insignificant, those "little things" and "humble beginnings" are the most important and valuable in life, for all things arise from them.

If you want a business, start with the belief that you can make it. Then, work on it with what you have. In the physical realm, everything progresses from something much smaller. The mighty Sequoia, in all its gigantic wonder, was once a seed cone that could fit in the palm of our hands. We know that the smallest and simplest of illuminated incandescence can spark the destruction of hundreds of acres of forests and, with it, entire populations. In the spiritual realm and space of the mind, some of the greatest things stem from the most trivial beginnings. A subtle inquiry or passion becomes the origin of a great invention, musical masterpiece, or inspirational novel. A small spoken word can move a nation to war or peace; a pure belief in the truth can lead to a spiritual transformation for all mankind; and the smallest primal urge can lead us down a path of shadowy darkness and corruption.

For every cause, there is a beginning, which is always followed by an effect. Have you given much thought to the magnitude of your beginnings? Do you know their prominence and significance? To understand and embrace its true value is to begin a valuable walk towards wisdom. Our beginnings often determine our outcomes, which always lead us to a given result. There are exceptions, of course. We all know that there are good beginnings and bad beginnings, all of which are eternally accompanied by the law of cause and effect—a reaping of what has been sown. A seed of thought or early path will eventually grow or lead to something that is either wrong or right. Nevertheless, we can (with careful consideration) evade wrong beginnings by pursuing the right ones, and in doing so, we can elude negative outcomes while enjoying the positive ones.

> As we begin to recognise this truth we understand the importance of what every day brings...a new beginning, a new opportunity to start anew. A second chance.

Now it's understood that there are some starts in life that we have no control over. In all cases, we have no power over the nature or environments we were born into or the positive or negative effects of people's free will around us. We cannot worry about these types of beginnings, no matter how difficult they are. Instead, we must focus only on those beginnings that we have absolute influence and authority over.

These beginnings are to be discovered in the kingdom of our very own thoughts and actions. They are found in our mental attitudes in a variety of situations that we're confronted with on a daily basis.

Have you given much thought to how you begin each day? What time do you wake up? How do you begin your tasks and duties? In what frame of mind do you come upon the sanctified breath of life of a brand new day? There is often joy or unhappiness that follows after the right or wrong beginning of a new day. The secret to obtaining joy is when every day is started in a way that is deliberate and accompanied with a keen sense of appreciation and gratitude.

> *Do not despise these small beginnings, for the LORD rejoices to see the work begin.*
> Zechariah 4:10

Winning in your backyard doesn't require much, but a routine of preparedness. Your mental health depends on what you do every day for your future life.

Get up at an early hour

The Weight We Carry: A Blueprint for Dealing with Life's Burdens

I have noticed a significant improvement in my overall productivity and well-being ever since I started waking up early. My routine now involves waking up at 4:00 a.m. and engaging in physical activities such as biking in the summer and indoor exercise in the winter. This change has positively impacted both my work performance and my personal life.

I have come to realise that even if our daily responsibilities do not necessarily require it, it is wise to make it our firm commitment to shake off lethargy and start the day with a powerful mindset. By doing so, we strengthen our willpower and enhance our spirit, mind, and body. On the other hand, if we succumb to sluggish self-indulgence by consistently sleeping in or spending excessive time in bed, we may fall into a state of unhappiness and even depression. This luxury of extended sleep comes at a price.

Similar to an alcoholic who believes that a drink will make them feel better, we deceive ourselves if we rely on lingering in bed to cure our bad moods, difficulties, or disorders. In many cases, our own lethargy is the root cause of our issues. Over time, if we persist in this behaviour, we may unknowingly drain our mental and physical vitality, sacrificing our overall happiness. Therefore, although it may seem like a small change, waking up early is the initial step towards setting the tone for a great day.

After rising early, get moving

Start your day by heading to the gym or going for a refreshing walk. Allow one foot to lead the other, guiding you towards renewed energy and the invigorating freshness of a new day. It is during this serene morning hour that we can connect with a sense of clarity and tranquilly in our minds and spirits. This inner stillness enables us to approach our issues and problems with a calm and focused mindset.

The early morning holds a spiritual allure, drawing us towards its quietude and offering a perfect environment for deep reflection. As you embrace the beginning of another day, you will be greeted by marvellous silence and a radiant sunrise.

This sacred time allows for profound contemplation and sets the stage for joy to permeate throughout our homes and endeavours. Every task and undertaking we embark upon throughout the day will be infused with a self-assured spirit.

By consciously embracing the idea that every new beginning, shaped by our thoughts and actions, has the power to positively impact our mental, spiritual, and physical lives, we embrace the sense of newness that life offers. It is through this intentional approach that we can experience the fullness of life and cultivate a harmonious alignment between our mind, spirit, and body.

Forgive others, forgive yourself

Do not dwell on the sins and mistakes you made yesterday. Doing so gives us very little strength or energy for living positively today. Never (ever) believe in the thought that whatever yesterday's transgression was or is can prevent you from living a righteous, pure, and good life today. Begin today correctly by living it better than yesterday. Press Onward. We all make mistakes. Ask for forgiveness from others, forgive yourself, and then go full steam ahead. Darkness has no greater companion than a self-loathing, unforgiven, or unforgiving heart. Paul writes in Philippians: "But one thing I do, forgetting what is behind and straining towards what is ahead, is press on towards the goal." Press on, dear friends, for life, love, joy, and new beginnings await you. If you do not harbour any regrets or doubts, your mind gets renewed, and that is winning in your backyard. No one can change the course of your day.

Guard and value your thoughts

We often underestimate the power of our thoughts and fail to recognise their profound influence on our lives. Our thoughts have the ability to shape our minds, emotions, bodies, and circumstances. They play a significant role in our health, relationships, and spiritual well-being, as well as our successes and failures. Our thoughts are valuable resources that hold spiritual implications, attracting blessings or misfortune. While it may sound mystical, the adage "What we think about, We bring about!" holds true. Negative thoughts breed negative results, while positive thoughts generate positive outcomes.

The Bible provides us with timeless wisdom on how we should direct our thoughts. Philippians 4:8 advises us to think about things that are true, honourable, just, pure, lovely, commendable, excellent, and praiseworthy. Our thoughts serve as the humble beginnings of our behaviours. It is essential to be mindful of what we allow to take root in our minds. Our thoughts, with their significant influence, shape our actions, which in turn produce the fruits of our character and ultimately shape our destiny. Therefore, it is crucial to eliminate negative thoughts and nurture only those that lead us towards righteousness and new beginnings that are good and virtuous.

Your backyard is the breeding and testing ground

It's fascinating to learn about President Obama's first job scooping ice cream at a Baskin Robbins in Hawaii. This serves as a reminder that everyone starts somewhere and that each experience we have contributes to our growth and development. From that early job, President Obama likely acquired important customer service and communication skills, which he continued to build upon throughout his career, eventually leading him to become the leader of our nation.

Many young people overlook the fact that every opportunity and experience has the potential to shape them. Each experience provides valuable perspectives and contributes to a transferable skillset. Transferrable skills, also known as soft skills, are highly valuable and applicable across various situations and fields. These skills include effective communication, leadership abilities, problem-solving capabilities, and strong interpersonal skills.

While door-to-door salespeople may be commonly perceived as bothersome and intrusive, it's important to challenge those perceptions. Reed Hastings, the Founder of Netflix, worked as a door-to-door vacuum salesman for 20 years before starting Netflix. In this role, Hastings likely honed his sales skills, which later became instrumental when he pitched his idea to investors. There are parallels between being a door-to-door salesman and starting a business, as both require creativity, the ability to sell an idea, and resilience in the face of rejection. It's worth remembering that our humble beginnings have the potential to shape us in profound ways!

Chapter Four

The Power of Anticipation

I appreciate GPS technology. By the way, I came up with this analogy while having tea with Arthur Masoma and Dezry Kay in Bryanston at a delightful restaurant called Paul. Unexpectedly, I overheard a conversation in the background among some Pedi individuals. They were debating what GPS stands for. It occurred to me that they could have simply Googled the answer. The argument seemed unnecessary, and none of them got it right.

This led me to ponder how GPS actually works and why so many people trust it, even without knowing its full name. It dawned on me that we had actually relied on GPS to navigate to the restaurant without questioning its accuracy. It's fascinating how anticipation plays a role. The first step when using a GPS is to input your destination. We entered the restaurant's address into the GPS, which then analysed the information, considered traffic conditions, and calculated the optimal route. As we embarked on our drive, the GPS provided turn-by-turn directions, guiding us on when to turn, which route to follow, and what to expect ahead. In the event of unexpected traffic or road closures, the GPS would recalculate the route and offer alternative directions. Following these instructions, we eventually reached our desired destination, successfully achieving our goal.

Now, I digress from my original train of thought. In this analogy, the GPS system represents anticipation, offering guidance and adaptability to help you effectively reach your desired destination. Similar to how a GPS system enhances navigation, anticipation empowers you to make informed decisions, overcome obstacles, and achieve your life goals. However, there was one instance when the GPS led me to a closed-down factory and claimed the signal was lost. I had to find my way out, and let's just say it wasn't a pleasant experience.

Many of us fail to fully experience what life has in store because we rely too heavily on anticipation. We anticipate work promotions without putting in the necessary effort. This anticipation often stems from factors like seniority, age, or being well-liked by the boss. We become complacent, assuming we deserve everything and that there is a guaranteed path reserved for us. On the other hand, someone else who anticipates a promotion might work diligently, striving to master their job and increase their chances of advancement. That, too, is anticipation. I hope you grasp the underlying point.

Blue Monday

The power of anticipation can have a significant impact, whether positive or negative. What are your anticipations in life? Each day brings renewed anticipation. For example, Mondays are often associated with a sense of dread or "Monday blues." This refers to the feelings of depression, tiredness, hopelessness, and the general unpleasantness of returning to work and routine after a weekend. Anticipating a bad day on Monday can trigger overwhelming feelings of anxiety, sadness, or stress, leading to a lack of passion and motivation on Monday mornings.

This negative anticipation can have detrimental effects on performance and productivity, affecting not only oneself but also those around them. Numerous studies in psychology and neurology have shown that our current emotional state greatly influences the quality of our work. When feeling blue, productivity and motivation decrease, pessimism increases, creativity declines, engagement levels drop, and learning becomes slower.

Unfortunately, many individuals have adopted this negative anticipation as a habit, resulting in consistently poor performance. It is essential to recognise the impact of our mindset and find ways to manage and improve it. By practising self-care, fostering a positive outlook, and implementing strategies to cope with stress, it is possible to mitigate the effects of the Monday blues and enhance overall performance and well-being.

Anticipation is a powerful force, and by consciously shifting our mindset and focusing on positivity, we can positively influence our experiences and outcomes, not just on Mondays but throughout the week.

Do you remember the Carly Simon song "Anticipation?" If you love Carly Simon the way I do you might enjoy her performance at this URL: http://www.youtube.com/watch?v=4NwP3wes4M8.

Humpday

There is an amusing commercial featuring a camel walking through an office, asking each worker, "What day of the week is it?" The culmination is when someone finally responds with "It's Humpday," causing the camel to burst with joy, exclaiming, "Humpday, Humpday." We can all appreciate the humour in the connection between Humpday and the camel.

However, the underlying message is that Wednesday, Humpday, signifies that the work week is progressing towards Friday, which is eagerly anticipated with great joy.

Friday marks the end of the work week, allowing everyone to look forward to going out on Friday night, sleeping in on Saturday morning, and enjoying the weekend. This is why the acronym TGIF, "Thank God It's Friday," has become so popular. In fact, it has even inspired a restaurant chain named after it. Thankfully, I have yet to receive this particular message on WhatsApp. My friends are unaware of it, and if they were, they would likely overuse it like other shorthand texts such as LOL, which I personally dislike.

Thank God it's Friday

If we look at the flip side, we encounter "The Sunday Night Blues" when there is a sense of dread associated with the upcoming week. The anticipation of starting the work week, waking up early, and facing the demands and expectations can elicit negative emotions.

While the concept of "Day of the Week Moods" (DOW) has been discredited as not applicable to everyone, there is still significance in the role of anticipation. Generally, anticipation is associated with positive emotions. Positive anticipation occurs when people look forward to something with excitement. However, in the case of Sunday, those who experience stress and anxiety may have negative anticipation about the week ahead.

It is possible that those who anticipate negative outcomes tend to be pessimistic, while those who anticipate positive outcomes tend to be

optimistic. Additionally, individuals who anticipate negative outcomes may be dealing with depression and anxiety.
For instance, there are many individuals who anticipate the upcoming week with enjoyment because they genuinely love their jobs and often feel optimistic.

The psychology of anticipation is fascinating. Have you ever eagerly anticipated something only to feel the opposite once it actually happened?

Anticipating positive events, such as receiving a birthday gift or looking forward to a beach vacation, can evoke excitement and pleasure. The waiting period before these anticipated events is filled with the joy of imagining what they will be like. Similar to a child waiting for their first electric train set, there is a sense of fulfilment in living through the imagination.

Positive anticipation also plays a significant role in human sexuality. The tension that builds during the waiting period intensifies the excitement of what lies ahead. Many couples experience this type of anticipation when awaiting the evening after fulfilling their daily responsibilities.

In fact, positive anticipation feels so good that some individuals choose to delay immediate gratification in favour of the anticipation that comes with waiting for something in the future. Research supports the idea that many people opt to delay actions in the present for the sake of anticipation and its accompanying positive emotions.

Returning to Carly Simon's song "Anticipation," here are a few relevant lyrics:

Anticipation, anticipation
Is makin' me late
Is keepin' me waitin'

And I tell you how easy it feels to be with you
And how right your arms feel around me
But I, I rehearsed those lines just late last night
When I was thinkin' about how right tonight might be

Anticipation, anticipation
Is makin' me late
Is keepin' me waitin'

Our lives are indeed intertwined with anticipation. It affects our emotional state, our motivation, and our overall outlook on life. Anticipation can bring both joy and sadness, depending on our expectations and beliefs. We work diligently because we anticipate the rewards and benefits it may bring. Conversely, when we anticipate no recognition for our efforts, it can lead to a sense of sluggishness and disengagement.

Is anticipation better than living in the moment?

Definitely. I I have a friend who is a medical doctor, and her life is filled with the beauty of anticipation. On one of her challenging days, she was worried about her tonsils, struggling to breathe, and fearful of undergoing surgery. She appeared distressed, and I felt at a loss as to how to comfort her.

The Weight We Carry: A Blueprint for Dealing with Life's Burdens

However, when I asked her about her plans and upcoming adventures, I witnessed a remarkable transformation. Her face lit up, and she came back to life. She enthusiastically shared her plans for a Christmas trip. It was the anticipation of the journey and the process of organising it that brought her immense joy. It wasn't solely about the trip itself, but rather the anticipation surrounding it.

This experience taught me that we don't necessarily need a better future or success to find happiness. We don't have to wait for external circumstances to align before living a fulfilling life. The mere idea of what we could become should bring us the greatest joy. So, what are you anticipating in your life? If your life were a film, what would be its storyline? Where do you envision your life in the next 10 years? Your anticipation will shape your life over the next decade. If you don't anticipate anything better, you may find yourself feeling miserable. But if you anticipate a bright future, you'll be excited about every year leading up to that anticipated future.

My friend reminded me of a novel I once read about someone eagerly anticipating a holiday. It made me realise the value of anticipation. It allows us to derive pleasure from something in the near future, even before the event actually takes place. We can anticipate an exciting new job, an evening at the theatre, or a well-deserved holiday after a demanding quarter. Anticipation is a delightful and thrilling emotion, and unlike happiness or fulfilment, it can be generated quickly and easily. All we need to do is think about something we're looking forward to.

I've learned that there are numerous benefits to anticipation. The pleasure derived from anticipating something enjoyable is often equal to or even greater than the pleasure derived from the actual event itself.

This is because in our anticipation, we create and idealise the future. From Tlou's WhatsApp statuses, I could see she was anticipating a dream holiday with pristine beaches devoid of litter and a market free from persistent sellers. In that anticipation, we can envision strolling through empty landmarks in a state of bliss and relishing dining experiences at quaint seaside shacks without any digestive distress.

> **LP Hartley famously wrote, The past is a foreign country; they do things differently there'. If the past is a foreign country, the future is a whole other planet.**

This anticipatory period can be enhanced by planning everything well in advance. You can derive hours of pleasure by looking through suggestions from your travel advisor. Weighing up the benefits of one hotel versus the other. Trying to think of whether you'd like to plan your daily massage for 3:00pm or 4:30pm. Cruising through pages of Booking.com comments to find the most charming little restaurants in the area.

With a longer anticipatory period, you can involve so many more people in the planning process. Perhaps you've always wanted to play a game of tennis with Rafa Nadal. With months to plan and anticipate the event, you've got plenty of time for the necessary negotiations and communications to be made, with an even greater reward waiting for you at the end. Even if the star turns out to be a bit arrogant and unpleasant in person, you still gain so much enjoyment from the planning. You can reach out to a plethora of travel agents, tour operators, concierge services, and special interest tour operators who will all give you a different perspective as you flesh out the details of your dream escape.

The Weight We Carry: A Blueprint for Dealing with Life's Burdens

Even in the journey of life, we do well when we think better. When you plan your future, you get excited about the possibility of becoming who you believe you can be.

Interestingly, in a study published this year in the journal eNeuro, it was found that when gambling addicts were asked to think about a positive future experience, such as an upcoming holiday, they were better able to curb their impulses and choose long-term gratification over short-term gratification. The study illustrated how anticipating a pleasurable future situation can help humans work through an unpleasant present situation.
By giving us something positive to "look forward to" in the future, we can build up the discipline and motivation to tolerate temporary pain or frustration.

So, from this study, we can see that by planning travel further in advance, we become more mentally prepared to tolerate difficult situations. How long will you travel towards your future? Like a holiday, what are your plans? Perhaps the difficult situation is the reason you felt you needed a holiday in the first place, which begs the question: do you actually need to go on the holiday to reap the benefits of planning it? Is anticipating travel and the mental boost it gives you to get through the tough times enough to make us happy and relaxed without the inconvenience of actually going anywhere? A journey to your future feels exactly the same.

In Alain de Botton's book, 'The Art of Travel', he references the protagonist Duc des Esseintes from J.K. Huysman's novel, À Rebours. The Duc is a wealthy, decadent French nobleman who loves imagining voyages to foreign lands. Like how many of us ought to imagine our future. He becomes enamoured with the finesse of Dutch painting but is disappointed upon arriving in Holland that the idyllic images he saw, were not reflected in true life.

The same way we may imagine a future full of bliss, when we work on it, we realise it is not as rosy as it appeared in our dreams. A picture taken in summer will show greenery, but what will you experience when you travel in winter?

Later, after reading a Charles Dickens novel, he plans to travel to London. While still in Paris, he buys a guidebook, visits an English bar and then a tavern, and heads to the train station. Before leaving Paris, however, he quickly decides that he would rather not deal with the discomfort of travelling all that way for potentially another disappointment, so he heads back home. He never leaves his estate again but continues to daydream about his idyllic travels. He spends his days surrounding himself with trinkets, souvenirs, and travel memorabilia, such as ship schedules and train timetables, and is content with the anticipation, rather than the reality of going abroad.

In the journey of life as we anticipate, we may stumble at humble beginnings, meet more curves than imagined, experience unfavourable weather conditions, etc. But does that mean we cannot continue anticipating a better future?
Des Esseintes' disappointment reflects the gap between people's expectations of travel and its reality, as well as the seeming purity of foreign cultures in art and the imagination. Des Esseintes concluded, in Huysmans's words, that "the imagination could provide a more-than-adequate substitute for the vulgar reality of actual experience." The actual experience of travel is often diluted by the realisation that what we have come to see could have been seen anywhere else. For example, you may be familiar with the disappointment of driving hours to see a much-lauded temple, waterfall, or market that falls short of the temples, waterfalls, and markets you've already seen.

The Weight We Carry: A Blueprint for Dealing with Life's Burdens

While travelling, we also have the ever-present anxiety that we only have a limited amount of time to derive enjoyment, as we will shortly need to pack our bags, check out, and fly home. Our appreciation of aesthetic elements lies at the mercy of perplexing physical and psychological demands.

So, in an attempt to keep pushing the boundaries of what travel means and what it is for, we must discuss the possibility that actually travel is not essential at all. The essential part may just be the anticipation, and perhaps by simply planning a holiday, we can become happier and more content than if we embarked on the trip itself. Perhaps the new era of travel is not travelling in the first place.

This means that we may not all achieve our goals. We may not arrive at the expected time. We might not accomplish what we set out to do. But, in the meantime, the thought of what we can do and who we can become keeps us grounded and optimistic. Consider the agony of seeing yourself as a failure for ten years. You might as well see the bright side of life and improve your mental health. Depression is the gap or distance between what we have and what we are expected to have.

By the way, I meant to ask: what do you anticipate?

Chapter Five

Be Your Chief Executive - Visionary

Many treasured things don't grow in comfort zones. Take an aloe vera plant, for instance. If it is watered too often, it dies. The soil of the *aloe vera* plant should be allowed to go completely dry before being watered. Whereas your most treasured roses would die if not watered regularly. Aloes grow well in rocky mountains and deserts. They don't need fertiliser. Yet they grow thicker, and aloe is one of the most widely used medicinal plants on the planet.

The larger portion of Dubai is desert, but the Arabs have managed to build a global number one stop for almost every destination. Either you're on a connecting flight or you just go there to shop. Imagine if they had left for other countries, chasing rivers and fertile soil.

There was once a fisherman whose livelihood depended on his catch. One day, he was able to catch only one small fish. The fish, in its desperation to live, says, "Please leave me, kind sir. I am small and of no use to you. Let me go back into the river, and I can grow bigger. You can then catch me and make more money." The wise fisherman replies, "I will not give up a certain profit for one that doesn't exist yet."

Big things are the result of repeated small activities. Let me explain how corporations managed to keep the vision intact. Even on a personal level, you ought to run your life like a chief executive.

The fisherman knows very well that tomorrow is a result of today's sum of seconds, minutes and hours. You cannot ignore a second in your life and expect to have more time. The expectation placed upon both you and me in today's economy is this: *do more with less.*

To actually do more with less, you and I must constantly reinvent ourselves and expand our own leadership capacity for our own development. Maybe we should start thinking of ourselves as an institution. I've always thought of myself as a brand, and I devised a business plan to propel me to the next level of effectiveness. As a business owner, I am my own CEO, and I have planned my life by setting goals for myself.

Let's talk about goal-setting so you, too, can start to see yourself as a great idea that needs to be developed into a large corporation. If you want to have a goal, you can set one for yourself or your company.

Vision

Many people make the mistake of setting out a vision that can be achieved. You find that your vision is to complete matriculation. After you have completed it, what else will you live for? Are you going to change your vision? Vision statements are future-based, and they are meant to inspire and give direction. If you are starting a company, your vision cannot be to make more profit because money is a byproduct of value. So, to thrive in the long run, businesses must remain focused on producing value.

Most small enterprises fail to make it to their first anniversary because they are founded on making money rather than creating value.

However, it's easy to lose sight of value creation and get side tracked by other things like profit margins, expanding your product catalogues, or competitors. To become a runaway success, businesses must have a purpose that unites and inspires people; "making more money" won't do the trick. As the author Simon Sinek said, "People don't buy what you do; they buy why you do it."

Your vision must be impossible to achieve. Let me give a few examples so you may understand why a vision should be a lifetime mission. Let's check this out!

NIKE

Bring inspiration and innovation to every athlete in the world. If you have a body, you are an athlete.

For Nike, it would have been easily possible to inspire every athlete in America, but the world—8 billion people—is a lifetime hustle. The dynamics change, socioeconomic status changes; competition intensifies; and trends outlive one another.

So, it is not just about the apparel, but a movement. Nike's vision statement has captured the hearts of millions. "To bring inspiration and innovation to every athlete in the world" sounds a little vague at first. It's Nike co-founder Bill Bowerman's addition that hits you right in the feels: "If you have a body, you are an athlete." Bowerman's statement staunchly stands up against body-shaming and is a powerful call for inclusion. And it's not hard to see how this shapes Nike's philosophy and marketing.

University of Limpopo

Finding Solutions for Africa!

In a continent with a population of 1.4 billion that is plagued by so much lack, a university in a rural area intends to solve the challenges of millions of people. Isn't it too ambitious? It is. But that is what a vision is supposed to be. Africa is losing the battle against extreme poverty. About 30 million more Africans fell into extreme poverty (living on less than R35 a day) when COVID-19 broke out in 2019. Before the pandemic struck, over 445 million people—equivalent to 34% of Africa's population—lived below the poverty line. Even then, this figure was almost nine times the average for the rest of the world.

This means that the University will have to work hard for a lifetime to find solutions to African challenges. These challenges are dynamic and need different solutions. The University's core business is teaching and learning, research, and community engagement. It means that the institution will spend its lifetime advancing its core business and attracting the right staff, investment, etc. to work towards reaching the vision.

You see, setting a vision is not about what you can achieve instantly or over a few years. It is a lifetime value you can create. It is a statement that succinctly describes the very existence of your organisation. There's nothing wrong with a vision statement that is daring, distinct, or even disagreeable. If a vision statement sets out a generic goal that anyone can agree with, it is likely to produce mediocre results.

A goal like 'delivering an exceptional experience' applies equally to a hospital, bank, or fitness club'.

Here's a quick breakdown of what to do when formalising your vision statement:

- Project over 10 years into the future
- Dream big, and focus on success
- Use the present tense
- Use clear, concise, jargon-free language
- Infuse it with passion, and make it inspiring
- Align it with your business values and goals

Mission

Since I asserted that a vision should be exceedingly difficult, if not impossible, to achieve, one might question the purpose of companies. Why should one invest so much effort in something that may never be accomplished? However, it is precisely the existence of your brand that ensures its longevity. Even without having fully realised your vision, your brand will continue to endure, serving as a compelling reason to persist for a lifetime.

This is why businesses create endeavours that can be pursued in the interim while striving towards the vision; these endeavours are known as missions. In essence, a mission represents the active pursuit of a vision.

Mission statements are focused on the present and serve to communicate to stakeholders and community members the reason for a business's existence (the vision) and its current standing. A brand's mission is defined and articulated through its mission statement.

For instance, in the case of the University of Limpopo, whose vision is to "Find Solutions for Africa," its mission statement is to be **A University which responds actively:**

- To the development needs of its students, staff and communities,
- Through relevant and higher quality education and training, research and community engagement, and
- In partnership and collaboration with its stakeholders.

The primary objective of a mission is to bridge the gap between present reality and future vision. In the case of the institution seeking to find solutions to African challenges, achieving this goal necessitates the cultivation of innovative thinkers among students, the empowerment of creativity within the staff, and fostering collaboration with communities, enabling contributions to be made towards solving these challenges, one solution at a time.

To actively work towards finding solutions, the institution will offer relevant and high-quality education, promote engaged research to identify the root causes of challenges, and involve individuals facing these challenges so that they may actively participate in sustaining their own lives. Such endeavours require a collective effort and partnerships focused on improving the world.

It is important to note that the mission should not be limited to a single direction but should take various forms to encompass all aspects of building the future envisioned. Consequently, missions may have multiple statements or connotations.

In essence, a mission serves as an explanation of the steps one will take to progress towards the vision. It outlines the necessary requirements to reach the desired destination. For instance, if the vision is to travel safely to town, the mission may involve acquiring a reliable car, understanding road signs, obtaining fuel, and so on. This is a simplified explanation for better understanding. One of those is setting goals.

Goal

Do you ever feel as if you're sleepwalking through life, unsure of what you want? Perhaps you know exactly what you want to accomplish but don't know how to get there.

This is where goal setting comes into play. Goals are the first step in planning for the future, and they play an important role in the development of skills in many areas of life, including work, relationships, and everything in between. They are the target at which we aim our proverbial arrow.

Understanding the significance of goals and the techniques involved in setting attainable goals opens the door to success.

In the words of Pablo Picasso:

"Our goals can only be reached through a vehicle of a plan, in which we must fervently believe, and upon which we must vigorously act. There is no other route to success."

Everything is described in the quote. In addition, goals are frequently set for a period of one to five years. They assist us in achieving our medium-term goal. Commitment (attachment to the goal), clarity (specificity of the goal), challenge (degree of goal difficulty), complexity (degree of goal demands), and feedback (progress) are the key principles of successful goal-setting.

1. Commitment

Commitment refers to the degree to which an individual is attached to the goal and their determination to reach it, even when faced with obstacles. Goal performance is strongest when people are committed, and even more so when said goals are difficult (Locke & Latham, 1990).

Once they're committed, if an individual discovers their performance is inadequate, they are likely to increase their effort or change their strategy in order to attain it (Latham & Locke, 2006).

When we are less committed to goals, particularly more challenging goals, we increase the likelihood of giving up.

A number of factors can influence our commitment levels (Miner, 2005). Specifically, the perceived desirability of a goal and the perceived ability to achieve it to be successful, you must possess the desire and a comprehensive understanding of what is required to achieve your goal.

2. Clarity

Specific goals put you on a direct course. When a goal is vague, it has limited motivational value. Goal clarity is positively related to overall motivation and satisfaction in the workplace (Arvey et al., 1976).

Set clear, precise and unambiguous goals that are implicit and can be measured. When a goal is clear in your mind, you have an improved understanding of the task at hand. You know exactly what is required and the resulting success is a further source of motivation.

3. Challenging

Goals must be challenging yet attainable. Challenging goals can improve performance through increased self-satisfaction, and the motivation to find suitable strategies to push our skills to the limit (Locke & Latham, 1990). Conversely, goals that are not within our ability level may not be achieved, leading to feelings of dissatisfaction and frustration.

We are motivated by achievement and the anticipation of achievement. If we know a goal is challenging yet believe it is within our abilities to accomplish it, we are more likely to be motivated to complete it (Zimmerman et al., 1992).

4. Task complexity

Miner (2005) suggested that overly complex tasks introduce demands that may mute goal-setting effects. Overly complex goals that lie outside of our skill level may become overwhelming and negatively impact morale, productivity, and motivation.

The timeframe for such goals should be realistic. Allowing sufficient time to work towards a goal allows opportunities to reassess the goal's complexity while reviewing and improving performance. Even the most motivated people can become disillusioned if the task's complexity is too great for their skills.

5. Feedback

Goal setting is more effective in the presence of immediate feedback (Erez, 1977). Feedback, including internal feedback, helps to determine the degree to which a goal is being met and how you are progressing.

Unambiguous feedback ensures that action can be taken if necessary. If performance falls below the standard required to achieve a goal, feedback allows us to reflect on our abilities and set new, more attainable goals. When such feedback is delayed, we cannot evaluate the effectiveness of our strategies promptly, leading to a potential reduction in the rate of progress (Zimmerman, 2008).

When we perceive our progress towards a goal as adequate, we feel capable of learning new skills and setting more challenging future goals.

After setting out your goals, you need to know what you are going to do on a daily basis to meet them, so you can work towards your mission and get the value (vision) you want. Hence, what you do on a daily basis contributes towards achieving the goals. The fisherman can catch a small fish every day rather than waiting for a big fish, not knowing when that will be.

What you do every day, every hour, every second, and every nanosecond contributes to your goal. Develop intentional behaviour and live a purpose-driven life. It is not easy to make every second count, which is why, more than having activities, successful organisations have values. Values help guide one's behaviour, conduct, and reason for working towards a goal.

Staying with the University of Limpopo's example, its values are: Accountability, Transparency, Integrity, Academic Freedom, and Excellence and Professionalism. It means the staff, students, and researchers need to remain professional every day with a spirit of excellence in order to meet the developmental needs of communities. How could one find solutions if they were not accountable for their actions with integrity? So, the values are a moral compass that guides the direction of the goal with a mission in mind.

Even with our own plans, we have to be intentional on a daily basis. You cannot fail to explain why you did certain things and why you did not; you have to account for every minute spent. Is every minute you spend contributing to your vision? Are your actions aligned with who you want to become, and will they build the value you want to create?

Know where your time actually goes

It is crucial for you to know exactly where your time is going. Peter Drucker wrote about this many years ago and found that most people make totally incorrect assumptions about where their time goes. When they actually go through the process of measuring where their time goes, they are shocked at the gap between their perception and reality.

At least once a year, journal your time for a two-week period, measuring how you spend every ten minutes of your time. This insight will help you make significant adjustments to how you invest your time based on your priorities. Best of all, your changes will be informed by the actual reality of how you spend your time, not just your best guess. My rule of thumb is that when I start feeling like I'm losing my grip on the results I want to see in my life, I start measuring my time using an app and then make adjustments. I even have a water drinking app, for I know routine is far more important.

Focus on where you can make a real contribution

The second way to begin to expand your leadership capacity to do more with less is to intentionally focus more energy on what you can contribute and spend less time focusing on exactly what you will do.

Leaders have a bias towards action, i.e., the doing part of the leadership role. You certainly can't stop "doing" things, but you can deliberately spend less time and energy on things that don't move the organisation forward on the key outcomes you are responsible for accomplishing. Spend more time making sure you understand what your specific contribution can be to a conversation, meeting, plan, or project.

As your focus on your contribution improves, you will have greater clarity about the impact that only you can have on your organisation. You'll begin to say no to good things in a respectful way, so you can focus on the best things. As I've put effort into this area of personal growth, I find myself more frequently saying, "I only have one thing I can contribute to this topic," or, "I'm not sure I have much to offer to that idea, but I'm confident in your ability to make it work." It's embarrassing to me the amount of energy I've wasted on having opinions about things that don't actually relate to the areas where I can make the greatest contribution!

There are many things that you and I might have opinions about that could be helpful; they might be good ideas, but they aren't our greatest areas for impact.

Clarify the difference between responsibilities and projects

A third way to begin to expand your capacity is to make a clear distinction between the responsibilities of your role and the projects that you manage. It is wise to actually have this written down somewhere you can see it regularly. As a leader of your own destiny, you're responsible for many things in an ongoing way. These responsibilities usually do not have a beginning or end.

Projects, on the other hand, do have a clear starting point and an endpoint. This distinction becomes increasingly important if you are expected to do more with less. If you are not careful, you'll lose track of your ability to make progress in areas of responsibility and constantly gravitate towards doing projects that are more achievable in the short term. Ongoing responsibilities are excellent areas for you to work on your systems and habits that have a cumulative impact over longer periods of time. I ask people to articulate their daily, weekly, monthly, and quarterly responsibilities, separate from the actual projects they are working on. Consider how you can grow a system for success in your areas of responsibility.

Define success in 100 day cycles

A fourth way to grow your capacity to do more with less is to focus and define the goals you will accomplish over a specific timeframe. I prefer moving forward in 100-day cycles. Research actually shows that it is very difficult to sustain energy for more than 100 days. What I do is actually spend one day a month thinking about what I will accomplish in the next 100 days, and I write that down in black and white.

Usually, I have no more than five or six areas of emphasis for the next 100 days. I think specifically and articulate exactly where each of these projects should be at the end of the 100-day cycle. In my notes, I have a start date and an end date. While this may seem simplistic, it is a critical cornerstone component of a system for success, and it enabled me to constantly focus my energies in the right areas over the long haul. The pressure to do more with less can cripple your effectiveness if you let it. Be smart about it. Run your life as if it were an institution—it actually is—and be its chief executive. You will have to account for or give a report at the end of the year.

Chapter Six

Let Go of Validation Seeking

Of late, seeking validation has taken on a new form on social media. We post pictures and update statuses to be noticed and liked. I have seen posts that did not even last 30 minutes because they received a small number of likes from people we didn't even know. As important as it sounds, a repeated activity gets deeply rooted in our being, and we start to believe that we are less beautiful, less attractive, and less important. We go to the extreme of taking pictures in water wearing mermaid clothes, spending time partying, excessively spending on clothes and trips, etc. Everything is content to us, and we end up depending on a certain number of likes to feel important.

When we're constantly seeking approval from other people, we're only paving the way for more anxiety and depression in our lives. We may seek validation from others personally, such as via conversation or groups. Most often, via today's technology, we seek validation online, such as in social media posts and engagements. Validation is a slippery slope. It begins when we seek other people's opinions on our decisions in life, and it becomes complicated when we depend on this validation and live our lives in the mode of "people-pleasing" and meeting others' expectations.

Not only does this disempower us, but it also adds more stress, anxiety, and depression to our lives. Based on Maslow's psychological studies, we need to meet our basic needs of safety, survival, love, and a sense of belonging in our communities. This will allow us to tend to our self-esteem and listen to our intuitive guiding signals. From here, we can cut the ties of depending on validation and instead forge our own path in life and thrive along the journey.

It all comes down to the idea of belonging in the world, in your community, in your circle of friends, and in your family. When we have the sense that we belong, our love for others and ourselves skyrockets. That love fuels our self-esteem, and it also motivates us to be better and do better in the world.

This builds up to what psychologists call "self-actualisation." This term refers to our own ability to realise our fullest potential and develop our skills and talents to serve that potential. In other words, it's our launch pad into limitless possibilities because we finally believe we are worthy of them and have what it takes to accomplish them.

How does this connect to outside influence and validation? Well, the psychologist who coined the idea of "self-actualisation," Abraham Maslow, believed that to achieve this highest level of awareness, our basic needs first needed to be met. Those include primary needs such as food, shelter, water, and safety, but he also included basic psychological needs such as a sense of belonging, love, and healthy self-esteem.

It's no surprise, then, that any gap in these basic psychological needs leaves us open and vulnerable to relying on others for validation. When our self-esteem suffers and we don't believe in our own power, we turn to our community for help. In every sense, this is a wise decision. After all, our communities are there to help support us and lift us when we're feeling down and out.

However, there exists a fine balance between asking for advice and depending on it to chart the course of our lives. When we begin to depend on this validation as the primary driver, we are turning over the power of our entire lives.

It is human nature to want to be liked and accepted. However, this often leads to people worrying too much about what others are thinking about them. This kind of excessive worrying can have a negative effect on your life. It can be so debilitating that it interferes with your ability to feel at ease with yourself and around others.

> *Care about what other people think and you will always be their prisoner.*

I have seen even the most talented and creative young people do well but suffer depression two years later. One issue is that they become TikTok sensationalists, gain followership too quickly, and start appearing. The status of a celebrity kicks in, and they get trapped in it. Every weekend is all about going out in designer clothes, dining, and being who you are. Some end up forgetting the craft that got them fame and no longer investing in it, ending up losing followership. Get in debt and stop being active on the very same platforms that got them liked.

The Weight We Carry: A Blueprint for Dealing with Life's Burdens

When we urgently aim to please other people, we're seeking approval for ourselves from outside sources. And whenever we reach for something in the outside world to give us what we should be giving ourselves, we set ourselves up for disappointment. We set ourselves up to live a life we don't particularly want but that fits with what other people expect of us. We don't dare take a chance on something that may bring on a disapproving stare or rank low on the social status metre. We do what's expected of us. We do what others want for us and from us. In return, we get their approval. You might be thinking, "Why not seek approval?" Well, the reason is that we only get it at the expense of knowing what we want and being our true selves. When we seek others' approval, we miss opportunities to learn how to approve of ourselves—even if others don't.

The Importance of Knowing Yourself

When others' acceptance of you impacts how you make decisions about where to spend your time, you lose awareness of what's important to you, what drives you, and what makes you happy. You might feel stuck at work you don't particularly enjoy and continue habits that are counterproductive. If this feels true for you, it's time to focus your energy on getting in touch with what really matters to you. Start asking yourself questions like, what do I value? What keeps me awake at night? How is it that I prefer to spend my time? Start to listen to what you really want for your life and align your actions with

> Without realising it, you may be negatively impacting your effectiveness by seeking others' approval.

your values, principles, and goals. When you live in line with what you value, your life becomes much simpler and more effortless.

Instead of making decisions based on what others will approve of, start making them based on what's right for you. When you make conscious choices about how to spend your time and are committed to doing what's valuable to you, you're able to create your own life.

> *Contrary to popular belief, you don't need to be—or appear—constantly busy in order to be successful. As an alternative, you can see success as a measure of doing what matters to you.*
> Moses Moreroa

Here are ten reasons why you should not care about what others think:

It's Not Their Life, So It's None of Their Business

People are entitled to think whatever they want, just as you are entitled to think what you want. What people think of you cannot change who you are or what you are worth, unless you allow them to. This is your life to live. At the end of the day, you are the only person who needs to approve of your own choices.

They Don't Know What's Best For You

Nobody will ever be as invested in your life as you. Only you know what is best for you, and that entails learning from your own choices. The only way you will ever truly learn is by making your own decisions and taking full responsibility for them. That way, if you do fail, at least you can learn from it wholeheartedly, as opposed to blaming somebody else.

What's Right for Someone Else May Be Completely Wrong for You

It's important to recognise that someone's opinion is often based on what they would do. This alone is the problem. What is best for somebody else can be the worst thing for you. What one person considers garbage can be another person's treasure. We are all so unique. Only you know what is right for you.

It Will Keep You from Your Dreams

If you are constantly worried about what other people think, you will never get where you need to go in life. You are going to have to do things that don't always meet people's standards. You will come into situations where you have to put your pride and your reputation on the line to get what you want. If you are constantly worried about what people are thinking, you will never have the will to do what's right.

You're The One Stuck with the End Result

In life, you are the one stuck with the consequences of your decisions. For example, if someone suggests you buy some stocks but you just don't feel like it's the right choice, you are the only one who will live with the consequences. If the stock falls and you lose a lot of money, you are the one who will have to live with the fact that you didn't follow your inner call. When people give you their suggestions or even orders, there is no risk for them. They don't have to live with your choices, but you do.

People's Thoughts Change on a Regular Basis

We are constantly changing. Some philosophers and theorists suggest that we are in a constant state of flux, so much so that we cannot even say we have one specific 'self' (or a fixed personality). People's thoughts, ideas, and views change on a regular basis. That means even if somebody does think badly of you at the moment, there is a good chance they will think differently in the near future. So basically, people's thoughts don't really matter.

Life Is Simply Too Short

You only have one life to live, so why would you spend it worrying about other people's opinions? Do whatever you want and be whoever you want. You're not going to see these people after you're dead. You probably won't even see them in a year. Live your life without worrying about other people's thoughts and opinions, and you will live your life to the maximum.

You Reap What You Sow

Worrying too much about what other people think of you can become a self-fulfilling prophecy. Frequently, people indulge their need to be liked so much that it actually dictates the way they behave. Some become people-pleasers or so submissive that many people are turned off. The behaviour you use as an attempt to ensure you are liked may actually cause you to be disliked.

Others Don't Care As Much As You Think

People generally don't think outside themselves a great deal of the time. It is a sad but simple truth that the average person filters their world through their ego, meaning that they think about most things in terms of "me" or "my". This means that, unless who you are or what you have done directly affects another person or their life, they are unlikely to spend much time thinking about you at all.

The Hard Truth: It's Impossible to Please Everybody

You can't please everyone all of the time. It is impossible to live up to everyone's expectations, so there is no point in burning yourself out trying to do so. Just make sure that one of the people you please is yourself!

Chapter Seven

Mastering the Basics of Life

Mastering the basics of life is like learning to ride a bicycle. When you first start, it may seem daunting and unstable. You wobble, lose balance, and fall down. But with determination and practice, you begin to find your rhythm.

Just like riding a bike, life requires us to learn fundamental skills. We need to understand how to navigate relationships, manage our finances, maintain good health, and cultivate personal growth. At first, it may feel overwhelming, and we may stumble along the way. However, as we persist, we gradually gain confidence and find stability.

Just as a cyclist learns to pedal smoothly, shift gears, and steer with precision, mastering life's basics involves honing essential skills. We learn to communicate effectively, adapt to changes, make sound decisions, and set achievable goals. These foundational abilities become the building blocks upon which we construct a fulfilling and purposeful life.

The Weight We Carry: A Blueprint for Dealing with Life's Burdens

Like riding a bike, mastering life's basics requires perseverance. It's not a one-time effort but an ongoing journey. We may encounter obstacles, setbacks, or unexpected turns.

However, by staying focused, being resilient, and continually learning from our experiences, we gain mastery over life's essentials, just as a skilled cyclist navigates effortlessly through different terrains.

Ultimately, mastering the basics of life is about finding balance, staying steady, and moving forward. It's about developing the confidence and competence to handle whatever challenges come our way. So, just as riding a bike becomes second nature with practice, embracing and mastering life's fundamentals enables us to navigate its complexities with grace and ease.

Do you find it difficult to find happiness and success in all aspects of your life? Perhaps your career has taken over your relationships, or your health has prevented you from participating in your favourite hobbies. In either case, when we lose our sense of balance in life, it's a sign that we need to reconsider our priorities and find a more holistic way of living. A method that takes into account our mental and physical health, our career, our finances, our relationships, and our spiritual well-being.

I'm not sure what mental health is or isn't, but I do know how to live a healthy life. I'm aware of a few things that could derail your life, big or small, and lead to a mental breakdown. I will not attempt to distinguish between normal mental health and mental disorders. Because when I asked for the distinction, I sometimes got a clear answer, but the distinction isn't always so clear.

For example, if you're afraid of giving a public speech, does that mean you have a mental health disorder or just a bad case of nerves? Or, when does shyness turn into social phobia?

Allow me to define it based on my own life experiences, with the goal of identifying at least a few important aspects of life that could promote your mental health and keep you sane in an uncertain world.

I'd like to believe that poor mental health contributes to our inability to master life's fundamentals, because mental health is the overall wellness of how you think, regulate your feelings, and behave.

Let's take a look at six (6) important aspects of life and how we can plan our success around them.

I'll explain each of the aspects in a moment, but first, I'd like you to spend a few minutes completing a *Life Assessment* to find out how balanced (or unbalanced!) your life is right now. The *Life Assessment* will help you understand your life better — enabling you to discover how to live your life to the fullest.

The Weight We Carry: A Blueprint for Dealing with Life's Burdens

This assessment will give you the jumpstart you need to begin your journey towards a full and meaningful life. This **Full Life Framework** will help you achieve these goals:

- To excel in not just one area, but all important areas of your life
- With practical ideas and actions that anybody can understand and practice
- Achieving all this while overcoming real world constraints.

Understanding where you stand now and where you want to be is the first important step in your journey. This survey consists of four (4) parts, covering a range of your life aspects, and will take approximately five (5) minutes. Just read the statements carefully, answer honestly, and you'll feel a little better!

YOUR PRIORITY

	High	Low
Eating healthy food		
Working out regularly at the gym or at home		
Getting 8 hours of sleep every night		
Keeping a balanced diet		
Doing meditation		
Relaxation through deep breathing		
Getting enough rest		
Doing regular exercise		
Taking care of personal hygiene		
Fostering a close relationship with my family		
Appreciate other people's presence in my life		
Refrain from judging loved ones		
Love unconditionally		
Give advice sincerely		
Being financial free in the near future		
Having the courage to take risks		
Having high level of resilience		
Able to focus on a task till completion		
Ability to control anger or impulse		
Having emotional stability to manage life stressors		
Having high confidence in myself		
Having the resolve to overcome obstacles in life		
Ability to persevere in all kind of hardships in life		
Accepting that life has meaning and purpose		
Having positive core values that determines our self-worth		
Having a clear career identity		
Establishing strong and good reputation		

YOUR LEVEL OF SATISFACTION	High	Low
My health		
My body		
My diet		
My stamina		
Amount of rest I am getting		
Frequency of exercises I am doing		
My level of physical energy		
Relationship with my parents		
Relationship with my significant other		
Relationship with my siblings		
Relationship with my close friends		
Relationship with my colleagues		
My level of care and concern for people in general		
My salary		
Money that I am saving		
My ability to generate extra income		
My plan to attain financial freedom		
My plan to start a business		
Me having manageable liabilities		
My budget and cash flow		
My monetary management skills		
My early retirement plan		
My current job		
My career prospects		
My scope of work and responsibilities		
My working environment		
Being grateful with my life		

YOUR STRENGTH & WEAKNESS	High	Low
Ability to rise up again after failures		
Being patient despite all odds		
A winning mindset		
Taking risks and chance in life		
Emotionally stable		
High level of perseverance		
Ability to manage stress well		
Having self-control		
Ability to speak up and defend the truth		
Being optimistic in life		
Ability to stay calm in stressful situations		
Being thankful with what I have		
My morals		
High spirituality awareness		
My preference for meditation or yoga		
Having a clear life purpose		
Ability to forgive others		
Ability to avoid temptations or sudden impulses		
Being creative in coming up with new ideas		
Being a good team player		
Being able to lead and take charge at work		
Getting work done on time before their due dates		
Being a potential entrepreneur		
Being financially ambitious		
Ability to diversify investment portfolios		
Making wise monetary decisions		
Being a positive influence in a relationship		

DISC PERSONALITY	YES	NO
Charming and adventurous		
Bold and result focused		
May appear arrogant and cocky to others		
Can appear to be interested only in their own advancement		
Aggressive and cautious		
Dynamic and driven		
Can appear aloof		
Skeptical and impatient with others		
Visionary and persuasive		
Energetic and creative		
Poor with routine		
Unrealistic and may change direction often		
Versatile and responsive		
Respectful and loyal		
Giving trust too quickly		
Too passive		
Empathetic and cooperative		
Social and responsive		
Hard to say 'no'		
People pleasing		
Careful and dependable		
Dislike change		
Will say yes to avoid conflict		
Establishes connections with other people quickly		
Easy to express feelings		
High expectation on oneself		
An analytical mindset		

I came across these aspects early in my career after I burned myself out by continually pushing myself—until my mind and body gave me clear signals to stop!

After my mental and physical health had been severely compromised, I lost the energy and motivation to keep going with my career. This also led to a decline in my self-confidence and a drop in my productivity and creativity.

However, it wasn't all bad news. I was able to use the downtime as a wake-up call. I realised that anything taken to the extreme is unsustainable and that a happy, healthy, and successful life only comes when all parts of our lives are in harmony and balance.

This was the impetus for creating the six basic aspects of life—aspects that need to be balanced and fulfilled in order for us to function naturally and optimally.

I'll talk now about each of the Life Aspects, plus I'll give hints and tips on how to maximise each area, including how to benefit from core skills that I've termed life multipliers.

1. Physical Health

Imagine having tonnes of drive and energy and being able to consistently achieve your goals and desires. This can be a reality if you spend small but regular periods of time developing and maintaining your physical health.

You can do this by making simple changes to your life, such as improving your diet, exercising more, and practising meditation.

These activities could lead to BIG gains in your physical and mental health.

And critically, your health improvements will also inevitably lead to gains in ALL areas of your life.

Life Multiplier: Develop renewable vitality. Through eating, exercising, and sleeping well, you'll be able to keep your energy levels at their maximum.

2. Family and Relationship Fulfilment

When you have happy and healthy relationships with friends, family, and colleagues, you'll also have the necessary foundations for overall success and well-being in your life. Harmonious relationships are so important that I recommend you limit the amount of time you spend with negative people and increase the time you spend with creative, enthusiastic, and supportive people. By doing this, you'll keep yourself in tune with success. Of course, I'm not suggesting you cut yourself off completely from any of your negative friends or family members, but you'll certainly benefit by reducing the amount of time you spend with them.

Life Multiplier: Learn how to master your emotions. This will enable you to get along with almost everyone. It also means that you won't be pushed around by life's ever-changing circumstances.

3. Work and Career Prosperity

For most people, their career is one of their top priorities. And this makes sense, as on average we spend around 1,800 hours per year working. Work is also the main source of income for the majority of people.

It's definitely a positive thing to focus on progressing your career. This will give you something to aim for, and it ties in with research that shows that striving towards goals makes people happier.

Life Multiplier: Learn the art of self-control. You can do this by building positive new habits that will support your goals and aspirations.

4. Wealth and Money Satisfaction

You've probably heard that money is the root of all evil. However, this is inaccurate. The full Bible quotation is "The love of money is the root of all evil."

It's normal and natural to want to have sufficient money to pay for you and your family's needs — including mortgages, cars and holidays.

However, don't put your focus on money; instead, put your focus on offering a service or product to the world. If it's something that people need and want, then you should charge fairly for it and enjoy the rewards.

Life Multiplier: Be self-empowered. With this quality operating in your life, you'll have the confidence to be a high earner; you'll also have the confidence to spend money on necessities and luxuries (we all need a treat from time to time!).

5. Spiritual Wellness

While I'm predominantly a logical person, I don't believe that every decision and action has to be based on facts and figures. Sometimes we need to follow our intuition and our hearts. Whether you believe there is a power greater than us or not, spiritual practices such as meditation, breathing exercises, and singing can help us tap into a world beyond logic.

It's also worth noting that research shows that people who believe in a higher power tend to be happier and more satisfied with life than those who don't. A colleague of mine, Lebogang Mokaze, has experienced most of my intuition decisions, when I randomly said, This doesn't feel right, and changed my mind. When I would say, "Let's leave this place, and something bad happens immediately after. I believe there is a higher power in all of us.

Life Multiplier: Discover conscious communications. This means being able to tune into others as well as have a higher perspective.

6. Mental Strength

I find it easy to spot someone with a weak mind: They have no focus, no discipline, and they lack conviction and drive. On the other hand, I also find it easy to spot someone with a strong mind. They are dynamic, purposeful, and engaging. They also quickly impress as someone who can 'get things done'.

Life Multiplier: Learn the art of smart focus. This will enable you to get things done in the most effective and efficient manner. When you have the power of smart focus working in your life, you'll have the necessary time and energy to develop your mental strength. Focus is the sum total of productivity and intelligence.

If you take your time to master these aspects of life, surely a new life awaits you. So now you have the keys to living a full and holistic life. You just need to take action and begin balancing all aspects of your life. You can do this by implementing the suggested *Life Multipliers*.

Pat Williams put it cleverly, in his question of 'what are you living for?' when he said:

"Money can buy a house, but not a home; a bed, but not rest; food, but not an appetite; medicine, but not health; information, but not wisdom; thrills, but not joy; associates, but not friends; servants, but not loyalty; flattery, but not respect."

The Weight We Carry: A Blueprint for Dealing with Life's Burdens

This simply means that the important things in life need a balanced investment. Do not be a kind boss but a cruel father, a gentleman in public but an absent partner. Some people work hard but can't take care of their health, and so on. I'm excited to have shared the information in this article with you, as I know that it can transform all aspects of your life for the better and help you achieve your goals and dreams.

"I learned a few years ago that balance is the key to a happy and successful life, and a huge part of achieving that balance is to instill rituals into your everyday life — a nutritious balanced diet, daily exercise, time for yourself through meditation, reading, journaling, yoga, daily reflection, and setting goals."

Gretchen Bleiler

Chapter Eight

The Placebo Effect

A little girl lived in a small neighbourhood with her mother. Their next-door neighbour was an old painter who had strived for greatness but never achieved it.

During the harsh winter, the girl fell ill. Her mother called a doctor, who prescribed certain medicines for the treatment.

However, the condition of the girl didn't get better; in fact, it got worse. Her mother began to observe that she would gaze at the window and speak out a number. As time went by, the value of the number decreased.

Her mother asked her about it. The girl replied that she would look at the vine outside and count the number of leaves on it. She believed that she would die the day all the leaves fell.

Her mother saw that only five leaves were left now. She tried to persuade her daughter from thinking such nonsense, but it was to no avail. Another leaf would fall, and the girl's condition would worsen.

Finally, a day came when only one leaf remained. The girl was extremely sick, and her mother felt helpless. The night was going to be a stormy one, and the girl felt that the leaf would be gone by the morning.

However, the next morning, she woke up to find the leaf still there. She was a bit surprised, but she still felt that the leaf would not last long.

But it did. It was there the next morning and the morning after. And the girl's condition improved with each passing moment.

Finally, there came a day when the girl was pretty much fine. Her mother came by her side and said that she had some news for her. She informed her that the old painter had died.

The girl was sad to hear this. Her mother said he did manage to create a masterpiece before his death. When the girl asked about it, her mother replied, "The leaf on the window. He painted it the night the last leaf fell."

The mind can have a powerful influence on the body, and in some cases, it can even help the body heal. The mind can even sometimes trick you into believing that a fake treatment has real therapeutic results, a phenomenon known as the *placebo effect*. In some cases, these placebos can exert an influence powerful enough to mimic the effects of real medical treatments.

For instance, Khalo and Moremogolo went to the doctor to consult about a headache. The doctor gave Khalo Panado a pill, and Moremogolo was given the same-looking pill, but it had nothing inside. Khalo was healed by the pill, while Moremogolo was healed by the positive thinking that taking the pill would heal him. That's a placebo effect. You are not actually benefiting from a real thing, but from your positive thinking about it.

When you harness the power of positivity, it's amazing the impact it has on your life. It makes every moment worth experiencing and every goal worth shooting for. By thinking positively, you just can't help but be optimistic, even when everyone around you is miserable. As a result, you are happier, less depressed, and more satisfied.

So, anything you believe with your whole heart becomes your last hope. Social media has become a pandemic for most mental health issues and depression. Even older people have taken their lives under the bad influence of social media, yet we believe that it is the reason for our existence. It is the last thing we do before retiring to bed and the first thing we do when we wake up. We now believe it is the closest ally in our lives. We get affected by social media to the core, and I think we now suffer from a compulsive disorder as a result.

Smartphones, Snapchat, Instagram, TikTok, and other social media technologies help you stay connected. You're born with the drive to connect with others. It's good for your physical health and psychological well-being.

But what if you find yourself becoming too connected to social media?

There's growing evidence to suggest that some individuals can develop a dependency on social media that's not unlike an addiction to alcohol or drugs. Their overdependence on social media has led to symptoms typically associated with substance use disorders.

The dopamine loop

Using social media can lead to physical and psychological addiction because it triggers the brain's reward system to release dopamine, the "feel-good" chemical. Dopamine is actually a neurotransmitter (a chemical messenger between neurons) involved in neurological and physiological functioning.

It's the same chemical our brain releases when we eat, have sex, gamble, or use our smart phones.

For some users of social media, their brains may increase dopamine when they engage with Facebook, Snapchat, Instagram, or other social media platforms. When a user gets a like, a retweet, or an emoticon notification, the brain receives a flood of dopamine and sends it along reward pathways. It feels wonderful, but it also acts to reinforce our need to satisfy the feeling next time.

This cycle of motivation, reward, and reinforcement is a "dopamine loop" that gets users seeking, looking for, and craving rewards and more of them. People nowadays use social networking sites as a coping mechanism to relieve stress, loneliness, or depression. That is their pill for dealing with the pressures of life and stressors. They think they feel better after being on social media, like a placebo effect.

Compulsive users of social media tend to isolate. They're chasing that constant reward system, which can lead to interpersonal problems such as ignoring real-life relationships, work or school responsibilities, and one's physical health.

In turn, they feel bad about their behaviour, and to escape that undesirable feeling, they double-down on their social media behaviour for relief. When social network users repeat this cyclical pattern of relieving undesirable moods with social media use, the level of psychological dependency on social media increases.

How much is too much?

How do we know if you're spending too much time on social media? Ask your friends or a family member for their opinion. If you're still unsure, try to walk away from using social media for a few days.

Remember, breaking any habit is a challenge. But if it feels really uncomfortable for you, that warrants attention. Some people can't spend five minutes away from checking their phones—be it in a formal meeting, while driving, when eating, or almost everywhere. Their contribution to real-life situations is poor; they have below-average interpersonal skills and are not critical thinkers because they're too obsessed with social media as their most important place. When reality hits, they are always left wanting and believe everyone is out to get them.

> **To determine if someone is at risk of developing an addiction to social media, ask these six questions.**

1. Do they spend a lot of time thinking about social media or planning to use social media?
2. Do they feel the urge to use social media more and more?
3. Do they use social media to forget about personal problems?

4. Do they often try to reduce the use of social media without success?
5. Do they become restless or troubled if they are unable to use social media?
6. Do they use social media so much that it has had a negative impact on their job or studies?

> A "yes" to more than three of these questions may indicate a social media addiction.

Need a digital detox? Five tips to unplug

A digital detox is an agreed-upon period of time where individuals, companies, families, or other groups pledge to put down their phones and step away from their computers so they can concentrate on conversation, activities, learning new skills, and just generally being more aware of the concrete world around them.

But we have to start somewhere. Try these small and realistic changes.

- Stop using your phone as an alarm. Instead, use an actual alarm clock. It's just as handy and can help you stay off your mobile device before bed.
- Turn off notifications. Do you really need Twitter and Facebook updates throughout the day?
- Monitor the amount of time you spend on your device. Apps like "Screen Time" and "Digital Wellbeing" can help you control your daily usage. Set a reasonable time frame and stick to it. Maybe only one hour on your phone after dinner? Try a morning routine without any technology. Start with just a couple of times a week.

- Stick to one device at a time; don't use your phone while watching TV, using an iPad, or using a computer.
- Try not to revert to your phone in awkward social situations. And don't check your texts while in the middle of a conversation.
- Above everything else, make sure you aren't answering a quick text or using the web when you drive.

Chapter Nine

Illusion of Control

There was a captain on a sailboat during a powerful storm. Despite the captain's experience and expertise, the roaring winds and turbulent waves create a sense of control that is ultimately illusory.

The captain may believe that by holding onto the steering wheel tightly and adjusting the sails, they have a firm grip on the boat's direction and safety. However, the uncontrollable forces of nature are the true determinants of the boat's fate. The wind may suddenly change direction, the waves may become overwhelming, and the boat may be tossed about regardless of the captain's actions.

Similarly, in life, we often convince ourselves that we have significant control over our circumstances and outcomes. We engage in certain behaviours, follow specific routines, or make meticulous plans, believing that we have the power to shape our lives exactly as we desire. However, unforeseen events, external influences, and other factors beyond our control can disrupt our efforts and render our perceived control illusory.

The Weight We Carry: A Blueprint for Dealing with Life's Burdens

Just as the captain on the sailboat must learn to navigate the storm by adjusting to the changing conditions, we must also recognise the limitations of our control and adapt to the unpredictability of life. Accepting that some things are beyond our influence can lead to a more realistic perspective, helping us make wiser decisions, manage expectations, and find peace in the face of uncertainty.

Tragically, there are people who mysteriously believe they can control everything. I'm not sure if they're atypical or just exaggerate their self-importance. But this phenomenon has been growing right in front of my eyes. I have a few friends who will go to unimaginable lengths to demonstrate their success and how well they are doing in relationships, at work, and almost everywhere else. They portray a perfect life and even borrow money to maintain a lifestyle they do not have.

It's no surprise that the 2000s appear to have it all. But, upon closer inspection, they come from deep rural villages, live in RDPs, and lack basic needs. But in townships and cities, they cut a successful figure and try by all means to maintain it. I am not going to talk about how they maintain it; you all know.

My point is that they have reached a point where they actually believe they are who they think they are. They are now oblivious to their own truth; they are in a state of delusion and illusion. They believe they have control over their lives and that everything is normal.

Self-deception can fool us into believing our own lies and even make us more convincing. There's Elizabeth Holmes, the biotech entrepreneur, who in 2015 was declared the youngest and richest self-made female billionaire. She now faces 20 years in prison for fraud.

Then there's Anna Sorokin, aka Anna Delvey, who pretended to be a German heiress and subsequently fleeced New York's high society of hundreds of thousands of dollars. And Shimon Hayut, aka Simon Leviev, the so-called Tinder Swindler.

What marks all of these people is not just the lies they told others, but the lies they must have told themselves. They each believed their actions were somehow justifiable and, against all odds, believed they would never be found out. Time and again, they personally seemed to deny reality and drag others into their scams.

You might hope that this kind of behaviour is a relatively rare phenomenon, restricted to a few extreme situations. But self-deception is incredibly common and may have evolved to bring some personal benefits. We lie to ourselves to protect our self-images, which allows us to act immorally while maintaining a clear conscience. According to the very latest research, self-deception may have even evolved to help us persuade others; if we start believing our own lies, it's much easier to get other people to believe them, too.

When we get to this stage, we only realise it when we look at the man in the mirror and realise that "*no mahn*," I don't have this and that. I am always in luxury cars and going on trips, but why can't I drive to the mall and buy food today? You then realise that you are not who you think you are.

We maintain the illusion of control for so many good, yet dangerous, reasons and motives.

Safeguarding the ego

Any psychologist will tell you that studying self-deception scientifically is a headache. You can't simply ask someone if they are fooling themselves, since it happens below conscious awareness. As a result, the experiments are often highly intricate.

Let's begin with the research of Zoë Chance, an associate professor of marketing at Yale University. In an ingenious experiment from 2011, she showed that many people unconsciously employ self-deception to boost their egos.

Moral sincerity

The use of self-deception to enhance self-image has now been observed in many other contexts. For instance, Uri Gneezy, a professor of economics at the University of California, San Diego, has recently shown it can help us to justify potential conflicts of interest in our work.

Delusions of grandeur

In all these ways, our brains can fool us into believing things that are not true. Self-deception allows us to inflate our opinion of our own abilities so that we believe we are smarter than everyone around us. It means that we overlook the repercussions of our actions for other people so that we believe that we are generally acting in a moral way. And by deceiving ourselves about the veracity of our beliefs, we show greater conviction in our opinions, which can, in turn, help us persuade others.

It will make sense to you for a little while, until you get so deep that your own illusions haunt you. This has the potential to cause permanent emotional damage and could lead to depression and suicidal thoughts.

Keep it clean because the illusion of control not only destroys you on the inside, but it also eats away at your potential and opportunities. When you project yourself as being at the top of your game while unemployed, you miss out on opportunities because people assume you have everything figured out. It is acceptable not to be okay. It is acceptable to admit your shortcomings to others in order to gain access to opportunities. Your relationships would be destroyed by the illusion of control. Because you are afraid that people will see you for who you truly are, you will begin to isolate yourself. You are actually afraid of living now, which is why you are depressed. Stop lying to yourself and start living your truth.

Chapter Ten

How You Live Is What You Leave

Leaving a legacy is like planting a tree. Just as a tree's roots dig deep into the ground and spread far and wide, our actions and accomplishments become the foundation of our legacy. The seeds we sow, in the form of our ideas, contributions, and values, take root and grow, shaping the world long after we're gone.

Like a tree that provides shade and shelter for future generations, our legacy can touch the lives of others, offering them guidance, inspiration, and support. It stands tall and strong, weathering the storms of time and reminding people of who we were and what we stood for.

Just as a tree's branches reach towards the sky, our legacy can extend beyond our immediate sphere of influence. It can branch out into different areas, inspiring innovation, sparking change, and leaving a lasting impact on society. It can be a beacon of hope and a reminder that one person's actions can make a difference.

But just as a tree needs care and nurturing, our legacy requires attention and deliberate cultivation. We must plant our seeds of goodness with intention, tend to them, and help them grow. By investing our time, energy, and resources wisely, we can shape our legacy in a way that aligns with our values and leaves a positive mark on the world.

In the end, just as a forest is made up of individual trees, our collective legacies create a rich tapestry of human history. Each one of us has the power to contribute to this grand story, leaving behind a legacy that will continue to grow, evolve, and inspire generations to come.

A couple weeks ago, a good friend of mine relayed to me his life motto. It was only in passing, but it was profound: "Be brief, be bright, be gone."

These are words that I've been mulling over since then: so simple yet so powerful—and truthful. I'm glad that I heard them, and I'm relieved that such people exist who spread these ideas. Essentially, this formula for success doesn't seek recognition, fame, or power; it doesn't seek to force a name for its own sake. The irony is that this motto defies all of the notions of power, fame, and 'legacy' that too many individuals see as the definers of achievement.

The Weight We Carry: A Blueprint for Dealing with Life's Burdens

Which leads me to my main point: what exactly is a true legacy? What defines it if not being recognised for doing great things? I know billionaires who would not even give R10 to a street beggar. Caterers I know would rather feed leftovers to dogs than hoboes.

I know people who own cars but would never give someone a ride in the rain because it would dirty their car. I know some homeowners who take advantage of their housekeepers. I know parents who enslave their children through black taxes and debt.

I am sure you know many others whose actions leave much to be desired but who present themselves in public as kind, generous, hardworking, and so on. They go around tipping waiters while their children are left without toys.

I'm sure we've all encountered such behaviour at some point. I don't want to go into detail. The point is that how you live your life matters not to the rest of the world but to the person next to you. Your legacy is what you leave behind as a result of how you live. The world's wealthiest person who abuses their family leaves no desirable legacy. Even if the organisation is profitable, the abusive leader leaves no better legacy to his or her followers.

Being kind, helpful, and compassionate is the best legacy you can leave.

Chapter Eleven

Self-Hate

Self-hate is like a dark storm cloud that hovers persistently above you, casting a shadow over your every thought and action. It's as if this cloud follows you wherever you go, raining down feelings of worthlessness, shame, and self-doubt. Just as a storm unleashes thunder and lightning, self-hate unleashes a barrage of negative self-talk and self-sabotaging behaviours, creating an atmosphere of despair and self-destruction.

Imagine this storm cloud as a toxic companion, constantly whispering harsh judgements and criticisms in your ear. It obscures your ability to see the beauty and potential within yourself, much like a storm cloud blocks out the sunlight. It's as if you're trapped in a perpetual tempest, unable to escape the torrential downpour of self-hate.

But remember, storms eventually pass. Just as the weather changes, so too can your inner landscape. By seeking self-compassion and practising self-care, you can begin to disperse the storm cloud and invite rays of self-acceptance and love to break through. Over time, you can transform the thunderous self-hate into gentle showers of self-improvement and growth, nourishing the seeds of self-confidence and happiness within you.

If not suppressed, self-hatred spreads to the outside world, fueling hatred for others. Some people take offence when it is not given. When someone accomplishes something, they talk about their previous accomplishments. They mention their qualifications after you graduate. You buy a new car, and they tell you about its flaws. They call the producer and ask what the criteria are because they have done so much in their lives but have never been called to an interview. They are offended when you post a Bible verse. You post a joke, and they assume you're mocking them. When you promote your work online, they accuse you of bragging and being arrogant. You argue your point, and you're told that you believe you know everything. They say you're uninterested and aloof because you keep quiet.

Such people have a lot of self-hatred. They will infect you with their low self-esteem if you pay attention to them. Nothing is enough in front of their eyes. People who recognise when something is wrong but are unsure how to correct it.

Self-hatred causes you to doubt your own worth because you constantly compare yourself to others.

Self-hatred prevents you from appreciating your progress because you're always competing, while neglecting your passion because you don't feel fulfilled. When you fail to smile when others succeed, you are robbing yourself of the energy you need to succeed. Jealousy is the quickest poison you can consume to kill your ambitions—self-hate.

People who despise themselves always find ways to criticise the decisions of others. Self-hatred is always emotional rather than rational, and it steals your own peace. If you blame more than you compliment, you're a jerk, and it's a shame because you can't control your rage.

Self-hatred is characterised by persistent feelings of inadequacy, guilt, and low self-esteem. People may constantly compare themselves to others, focus on the negative while ignoring the positive, and believe they will never be "good enough." But everyone has worth and value, as well as the ability to cultivate self-love.

Self-loathing is excruciatingly painful, and there is no cure other than self-correction. How do you make corrections? Simply put, mind your own business. You will be depressed if you do not mind your own business.

At its core, minding your own business means focusing on what you can control and letting go of what you can't. It is accepting responsibility for one's own thoughts and actions while allowing others to accept responsibility for their own thoughts and actions.

So often, we try to control other people, the world around us, and everything and everyone except ourselves. The only thing we CAN control, ironically, is ourselves. Even so, it is an imperfect control.

Remember:

Your thoughts and actions = your business.

Other people's thoughts and actions = their business (NOT your business).

External circumstances (weather, external events, etc.) = NOT your business.

Take responsibility for YOU

Taking responsibility for yourself means knowing that no one makes you do or feel anything. It's not letting someone else have authority over you. You always have a choice. Minding your own business means choosing not to be the victim and completely taking ownership of your decisions.

Don't believe every thought in your head

When we mind our own business, we save a lot of energy because we are focused on what we want instead of what we don't want.

I like to think of it as sorting the mail.

Consider how much energy it takes to sort through all of the junk mail, special offers, fine print, and sales flyers. It would take the entire day! Instead, most of us take a quick look through the mail each day to see what really needs our attention, and then recycle or throw out the rest. Self-hatred is snooping around in other people's lives. You're curious about what they're doing on their computers. You're curious about what they're eating. You're curious about how they accomplished certain feats. You'd like to know everything about their lives. Stop! Determine what is important to you and your life.

Practice self-awareness

Minding your own business means observing what's going on inside of you. It's being self-observant. It may be helpful to think of ourselves as two "selves": the part of us that thinks and the part of us that can observe the part that thinks.

We can observe ourselves, our activity, and our state of mind. Minding your own business means being a self-observer. When you think a thought, you can automatically believe that thought, or the observer can watch your thought and say, "That's junk mail. No need to open that thought." You don't need to believe every thought you have. Most thoughts don't need to be believed. Do not believe your thoughts that everyone is against you—that's self-hate because you will never get peace. You will be depressed by your own thoughts.

Chapter Twelve

Sometimes It's Not About You

Thinking everything is about you is like standing in the centre of a crowded room with a mirror in hand. As you look around, every conversation, every interaction and every gesture is reflected back at you, making you believe that they are all somehow directed towards you. It's as if you wear tinted glasses that distort reality, making it difficult to see beyond the boundaries of your own perception.

In this self-centred mindset, it's like assuming that the rain falls just to dampen your spirits, that the laughter of others is meant to mock you, or that a frown from someone across the room is a judgement solely aimed at your existence. You interpret the world through the lens of your own ego, filtering out alternative explanations or considerations and attributing personal significance to every event or circumstance.

Much like the mirror you hold, this distorted perspective creates a reflection that is skewed, incomplete and ultimately disconnected from the bigger picture. It hampers your ability to empathise with others, understand their unique experiences and appreciate the multifaceted nature of the world around you.

Breaking free from self-centeredness requires setting aside the mirror, removing the tinted glasses, and embracing a more humble and open-minded outlook. It involves recognising that people have their own lives, concerns, and motivations that may have nothing to do with you. By shifting the focus away from yourself and cultivating a genuine curiosity about others, you can start to see the richness and diversity of human existence beyond the confines of your own perception.

Even the worst nightmares can be better than reality. You wake up and realise that it is not so much you who has changed as it is the people you once considered friends or even lovers who have now relegated you to the footnotes of their daily diaries of important stuff.

So, sometimes it's not about you being wrong but taking the wrong decisions.

There will be times when you realise that your life is yours to live. Don't plan it around anyone who isn't blood related, because if it goes wrong, they won't care. You can't blame them; they were only interested in surviving. Their grand plan is to thrive now that they have survived, and your role ends there. You couldn't thrive because they needed to survive, and you used resources you didn't have to keep them afloat. They will begin to think less about you, become fascinated by new people they meet, make you feel bad about yourself, dislike the things they once encouraged you to invest in, and when you compete for a place in their hearts, they will remind you that whatever you did was your choice and was never good enough. I have to agree that there were no lies detected; it was your decision to prioritise them. You should have loved yourself more, because you are all you have. *Motho o ka se mo confirme.* You ought to have listened to Makhadzi. *Ba tla go hurda!* So, almost all of the people who confront financial distress buckle under emotional hubbub, experience a dire

The Weight We Carry: A Blueprint for Dealing with Life's Burdens

lack of courage, exhibit pitiable performance, show a lack of vision, undergo waning hope, toss and turn between excessive resentment, and experience this because they put someone first, They wanted to impress and show their affection. If you don't let them be, they will not spare any of your brawls but hurt you even more as they strive to protect their new interests. Letting them be is not just about giving them what they deserve but also about freeing yourself from what you no longer deserve. Everything has an expiration date; yours might have just come a bit earlier than you thought. It is what it is, *yekela*! If they push you away, remember that in those moments, that's when you find yourself. We often meet people we don't deserve, and they teach us that any investment that is not for ourselves is insecure. You will be devastated, overwhelmed, and frustrated; that is exactly how you will heal. *The grief process is a healing process.* It was built into our systems to help us cope with the numerous losses we experience in life. If we trust the process fully, we will heal. Trusting the process means allowing the feelings to be what they are. Feelings are never wrong or bad. What we do because of feelings can be wrong or bad, but that is a choice. The feelings themselves are not bad. Therefore, they won't hurt us. They help us heal. If you trust this healing process, you will finally reach a point of acceptance. This is the point where decisions can be made and action can be taken. At this point, you are able to think clearly about the situation and decide what the best course of action is. And, of course, that action will vary depending on the person and the situation. You may decide that a continued relationship with this person can only lead to more hurt and is not worth the effort of trying to sustain a relationship. Or you may decide that there are too many good things in the relationship to give it up. As you decide, study their behaviour. Before you give it a try, observe little things, like hearing what they are not saying. If they make you feel less valued, it will never work because it means they want someone else to do what you are doing. It will never work if they hardly say *thank you*; it means they don't value your effort. It will never work if one little mistake cancels out the good moments; it means it wasn't a big deal for you. It will never work if they don't accept that what they do to you should be done to them; they're too controlling. It will never work if they first look for wrongs in you before praising your little rights, because blame is the emotional rival of compassion.

Sometimes you fall for someone who can't return the favour, and sometimes you're on the other side of that. Relationships are not based on just one person's needs; they will never work if you are considered the only responsible party. But this helps because the way to find yourself is to lose yourself in the service of others. I am not saying people should not wrong you, but they cannot always do it; it is toxic. One of the joys of being human is that we don't have to be perfect to be good. At some point, we will all make stupid decisions, hurt the people we love, say things that are hard to take back, and push too hard to get our way. None of that makes us toxic. It makes us human. We mess things up, we grow, and we learn. *Toxic people are different. They never learn. They never self-reflect, and they don't care who they hurt along the way.* It is no accident that they (toxic people) choose those who are open-hearted, generous, and willing to work hard for a relationship. With two non-toxic people, this is the foundation for something wonderful, but when toxic behaviour is involved, it is only a matter of time before that open heart becomes a broken one. If you are in any sort of relationship with someone who is toxic, chances are you have been bending and flexing for a while to try to make it work. *Stop. Just stop.* You can only change the things that are open to your influence, and toxic people will never be one of them.

7 Versions of Toxic People

1. **The Controller**

    Nobody should have to ask for permission or be heavily directed on what to wear, how to look, who to spend time with, or how to spend their money. There's nothing wrong with being open to the influence of the people around you, but 'the way you do it is for you to decide. Your mind is strong and beautiful and shouldn't be caged. Healthy relationships support independent thought. They don't crush it.

2. **The Taker**

    All relationships are about give and take, but if you're with a taker, you'll be doing all the giving and they'll be doing all the taking. To give is a gesture greater than the weight of a gift. A simple wallet for a guy goes a long way. A mere earing for a lady means the world. What do some of you call it—that it is the thought that counts, right? Emotionally, are they present, or do they hardly allow you to breathe?

    Think about what you get from the relationship. If it's nothing, it might be time to question why you're there. We all have a limited amount of resources (emotional energy and time) to share between our relationships. Every time you say 'yes' to someone who doesn't deserve you, you're saying 'no' to someone who does.

Give your energy to the people who deserve it, and when you're drawing up the list of deserving ones, make sure your own name is at the top.

3. The Absent

These versions of toxic people won't return texts or phone calls and will only be available when it suits them, usually when they want something. You might find yourself wondering whether they got your message, whether they're okay, or whether you've done something to upset them. No relationship should involve this much guesswork. If you don't believe me, go off social media for a day. It is uncommon and unusual for you; someone who cares should be calling to find out if you are okay. Let me not go far with this; I know it has already upset many of you.

4. The Manipulator

In my life, I have had to listen to people lie to me and allow them to continue thinking that I was getting a fair deal. You know when you are being fooled, but they don't know that you know. Manipulators will steal your joy as though you made it especially for them. They'll tell half-truths or straight-out lies, and when they have enough people squabbling, they'll be the saviour. 'Don't worry. I'm here for you.' Ugh. They'll listen, they'll comfort you, and they'll tell you what you want to hear. And then they'll ruin you. They'll change the facts of a situation, take things out of context, and use your words against you.

The Weight We Carry: A Blueprint for Dealing with Life's Burdens

They'll calmly poke you until you crack, then they'll poke you for cracking. They'll 'accidentally' spill secrets, or they'll hint that there are secrets there to spill, whether there are or not. There's just no reasoning with a manipulator, so forget trying to explain yourself. The argument will run in circles, and there will be no resolution. It's a black hole. Don't get sucked in.

When they are wrong, they will never admit it. This is them telling you, "I won't change for you. I feel better this way, even if it hurts you."

They do so well with reverse psychology. They will play victim and claim that someone always wants to make them look bad. A scenario would be:

You: *I feel like you're not listening to me.*
Them: *Are you calling me a bad listener?*
You: *No, I'm just saying that you've taken what I said the wrong way.*
Them: *Oh. So now you're saying I'm stupid. I can't believe you're doing this to me.*
You: *I am sorry.*
Them: *Don't be, I am always wrong.*

They'll only hear things through their negative filter, so the more you talk, the more they'll twist what you're saying. They want power, not a relationship. They'll use your weaknesses against you, and they'll use your strengths—your kindness, your openness, and your need for stability in the relationship. If they're showing tenderness, be careful; there's something you have that they want. Show them the door, and lock it when they leave.

5. The Attention Seeker

It's nice to be needed. But too much of everything is dangerous. Your world cannot stop whenever they are around you. Affection is great, but it doesn't mean you want it all the time. The attention seeker always has a crisis going on, and they always need your support. Be ready for aggression, passive aggression, angst, or a guilt trip if you don't respond.

'Oh. You're going to dinner with friends? It's just that I've had the worst day, and I really needed you tonight. Oh well, I suppose I can't always expect you to be there for me. If it's that important to you, then you should go. I just want you to be happy. I'll stay home alone and watch television or something (sigh). You go and have fun with your friends. I suppose I'll be okay.' See how that works? When there's always a crisis, it's only a matter of time before you're at the centre of one.

6. The One Who Wants to Change You

As they try so hard to change you, once you change, they will label you as weak. When you don't fight, they say you don't care. When you fight, they say you don't love them; it's a Catch-22.

It's one thing to let you know that the adorable snort thing you do when you laugh isn't so adorable, but when you're constantly reminded that you aren't smart enough, good-looking enough, skinny enough, or strong enough, you have to start thinking that the only thing that isn't good enough about you is this loser who keeps pointing these things out. You'll never be good enough for these people because it's not about you; it's about control and insecurity—

theirs, not yours. As long as they're working on changing you, they don't have to worry about themselves, and as long as they can keep you small, they'll have a shot at shining brighter. These people will make you doubt yourself by slowly convincing you that they know best and that they're doing it all for you. *'You'd just be so much prettier if you lost a few pounds, you know? I'm just being honest.'* Ugh. Unless you're having to be craned through your window or you're seriously unhealthy, it's nobody else's business how luscious your curves are. If you feel heavy, start by losing the 160 pounds of idiot beside you, and you won't believe how much lighter you'll feel.

These ones aren't looking out for you; they're trying to manage you. The people who deserve you will love you because of who you are, not despite it.

7. **The Jealous One**

Your partner is important, as are other people in your life. If you act in a trustworthy way, you deserve to be trusted. We all get insecure now and then, and sometimes we could all do with a little more loving and reassurance, but when the questions, accusations, and demands are consistent and without reason, it will only be a matter of time before your phone is checked, your movements are questioned, and your friends are closed out. Misplaced jealousy isn't love; it's a lack of trust in you.

Being human is complicated. Being open to the world is a great thing to do—it's wonderful—but when you're open to the world, you're also open to the poison that spills from it. One of the things that makes a difference is the people you hold close. Whether it's one, two, or a squadron-sized bunch, let the people around you be ones who are worthy of you.

***

Never blame anyone in your life. The good people will give you happiness. The bad people have experience. The worst people teach you a lesson. But the practical part of the lessons involves you suffering a lot. You go through many things that no one knows about. Whatever it was, it made you cry. It made you weak. It made you lay in bed all day, hoping that when you woke up, it was all gone. But in all honesty, we are mostly bothered by how other people treat us, not how we treat them. The best people give you memories.

***

Here is a note to myself: Stop seeing only the good in people and pay attention to what they show you. There are people who always want to change the bad narratives to something hopeful, even when people constantly disappoint, deceive, and hurt them and betray, undervalue, and devalue them. You keep convincing yourself that they don't really mean what they say.

But the thing is, some people hurt others to feel better about themselves. A boss who exploits, mistreats, and degrades his or her staff wants to nurture their egos, fears, and insecurities and hide the real issues affecting them.

All of us make mistakes. None of us is perfect. But watch and listen to how they immediately react. That will tell you if it's really a mistake or if they just love hurting you. This is a true reflection of someone's character. Actions speak louder than words.

It is time to stop seeing only the good in people and start focusing on what they really want to show you. They will start by disrespecting and openly attacking you. They will try by all means and, constantly, put you down. They start to emotionally harass you and do everything

The Weight We Carry: A Blueprint for Dealing with Life's Burdens

to make you feel uncomfortable, unsure, uncertain, confused, angry, and sad. It is your choice who you let into your life and what you let them do to you. The people who surround us should bring out the best in us. They should inspire us, motivate us, lift us, and not make us doubt ourselves.

But some of us are stuck with emotionally unavailable people who cannot commit to anything other than what benefits them. They tell you all you want to hear because it helps them get what they want.

Manipulators know how to weaken you and shake your self-confidence by distorting your perceptions of reality and making you sound like you're too far behind. These are people who clearly know your deepest insecurities and take advantage of them.

Some of these people always belittle their accomplishments. They put you down by making themselves seem superior. This is pure jealousy. They would die to be you. And if they had a chance, they would harm you to get what they wanted. People want to see you do well, but not better than them. They won't allow you to surpass their best level. When they show you the signs, take them as they are. When they hate you, be hateable.

Don't tolerate all these! Anyone who makes you feel bad about yourself doesn't deserve to be a part of your life.

You can't control how other people receive your energy.

Ever heard of the saying that anything you do or say gets filtered through the lens of whatever they are going through at the moment? Do not beat yourself up too hard when you're hated. Hate comes from a deep place. It's not you; it's them. It has nothing to do with you, but with them. The most important progress and success can't be seen. If you can validate yourself internally, then external validation becomes a byproduct.

You have to start forgiving yourself for the time you've wasted on things that never mattered. Forgive yourself for giving second chances to people who once took you for granted.

Forgive yourself for giving up on your dreams instead of working on them and making them come true because someone said you were not good enough.

And you have to forgive yourself for every second you spent not smiling, laughing, or living because someone said you did not look the part, that you did not fit in, that you lacked courage, and that you were not cut for being what you've always dreamed of becoming.

Not everyone is going to be right for you, want what's best for you, and help you realise your full potential. Don't resent them. Just forgive yourself for trusting that much and having higher expectations from people with low self-esteem who are engrossed in exaggerating their self-importance.

Chapter Thirteen

It Begins With You

Imagine entering a pitch-black room, unsure of what lies ahead. In your hand, you hold a tiny spark, barely visible but filled with immense potential. As you summon the courage to light it, the room gradually illuminates, revealing the path that was once hidden.

So, what would you do if you were not afraid? I've realised that even the most talented and gifted people rarely achieve success in life. Most highly gifted people live in a comfort zone, afraid of reaching their full potential and pretending to be successful while actually fearing more success.

Most successful millionaires, football players, musicians, actors, and others have not advanced in their education because those who are highly deserving are gripped by fear. The most famous people on the internet are not graduates of media studies programmes. The majority of caterers have never attended culinary school. The majority of entrepreneurs have not studied business. The best hangouts aren't run by hospitality or tourism graduates. Many talented beatmakers have not studied sound engineering or music. The majority of filmmakers have not studied film production or cinematography.

I see a lot of photographers making it big in malls and on the streets; some are now shooting music videos and planning high-profile events despite having never attended a photography school.

It's so sad that people fear success while simultaneously fearing failure. Are your greatest fears preventing you from achieving your greatest goals? People who hold themselves to high standards may unintentionally undermine their own success by fearing failure, rejection, or vulnerability. However, with some daily practices and mindset shifts, you may be able to turn your greatest fear into one of your greatest assets. You're probably interested in confronting whatever is holding you back, whether it's self-improvement, entrepreneurship, or achieving a big goal.

There are a few common fears that can bring any intelligent person to their knees because fear in highly gifted people masquerades as stress. Stress is the most obvious reaction to fear. This is how our brains detect danger and shift into "fight or flight" mode. The amygdala is responsible for a large portion of this reaction. Some people may have moved to better jobs, but their move is always associated with a negative connotation. They are afraid of starting over, of being in a new environment, and so on. I've seen subordinates rise above their line managers because they were not afraid to take advantage of new opportunities.

What if you didn't freak out? Panic attacks can occur when intense anxiety causes physical reactions. These are frequently in response to intangible and fictitious situations that feel very real inside your head.

What if you didn't have any phobias? Fears of snakes, spiders, germs, agoraphobia (wide open spaces), claustrophobia (confined spaces), and ghosts are among the most common.

Fear, in whatever form it takes, can feel like an impenetrable mental prison. Fear causes self-imposed limits, negative thoughts, low self-esteem, and self-doubt. Instead of seeing all of the possibilities, fear takes over your vision and sends the message to your brain that these things may harm or even kill you.

Fear of failure

We've all heard motivational speeches about failure. Thomas Edison conducted over a thousand failed experiments before he finally completed the light bulb. Denzel Washington received a lot of rejections after auditioning for dozens of plays and movies before getting a role.

These are grand, obvious examples that successful people can delineate in hindsight. But when you look at your own life, a fear of failure may disguise itself as:

- Setting goals that are too easy to attain
- Setting goals that are too high so you aren't hurt if you don't accomplish them
- Creating low expectations for yourself
- Avoiding new hobbies, sports, or career endeavours (sticking with what you know)
- Hiding your creative talents
- Coming up with lots of ideas and never executing them
- Getting easily discouraged by setbacks and giving up too soon
- Perfectionism (working forever to "make something perfect" as a means of procrastination because you don't want the project to be a failure)

Fear of failure keeps you in your comfort zone. It prevents you from doing anything your brain thinks is risky.

Fail at something everyday

How to Overcome It: Overcoming the fear of failure sounds nice in inspirational quotes, but how do you beat this fear every day?

Try the *"Fail at Something Everyday"* Method. This is perfect for someone who disguises their fear of success as a fear of failure. If you've always been good at what you do, you're probably staying in that comfort zone because it feels good. You like winning, and you don't have many losses under your belt.

The premise is simple: do something every day that you can fail at. Sounds painful, right?

This process can boost your confidence because it helps you build resilience to failure. Awkwardly trying something, embarrassing yourself, and laughing it off are crucial steps to sharpening your failure sword. You're trying something awkward every day and getting used to the feeling of sucking.

Most people are afraid to be bad at something, so they never try. Denzel Washington said it best—you will be bad at something, so why not practise building up your failure immunity in advance?

The Weight We Carry: A Blueprint for Dealing with Life's Burdens

His infamous speech at the University of Pennsylvania went like this:

> You will fail at some point in your life. Accept it. You will lose. Embarrass yourself. You will such at something. There is no doubt about it.
>
> I was a 1.8 GPA one semester and the university, very politely, suggested that it might be better to take some time off. I was 20 years old. I was at my lowest point, but here is a thing: I didn't quit. I didn't fall back, but I continued to fail and fail.
>
> But it didn't matter because you know what, there's an old saying: you hang around the barbershop long enough sooner or later you're going to get a haircut.
>
> So, you will catch a break, I did catch a break.
>
> Last year, I did a play called Fences on Broadway, he was at the same theatre that I failed that firs audition 30 years prior.
>
> Thomas Edison conducted 1000 failed experiments and you that haughty moment because the 1000 and first was the light bulb. Sometimes it is the best way to figure out where you're going. Never be discouraged. Never hold back.
>
> Give everything you've got and when you fall throughout life, remember this: all fall – fail forward.

Fear of Rejection

The fear of rejection is among the most common fears in the world. Science tells us that rejection and physical pain signal the same pathways in our brains.

It's no surprise that getting rejected is one of the most ancient fears among our species. In the primal part of your brain called the limbic system, or "lizard brain," any form of denial or exclusion sounds an alarm: your tribe has left you behind to fend for yourself. The next thing you know, you're in "fight or flight" mode. Stress and loneliness skyrocket, while motivation and self-esteem plummet.

Whether you're dealing with social awkwardness, letting go of someone who doesn't want to be your friend, or getting denied an essential professional opportunity, remember that everyone has gotten rejected at some point in their life. For example, J.K. Rowling's Harry Potter manuscript was rejected by 12 different publishing houses before she finally found a publisher for the book. You can conquer this fear of rejection by boosting your confidence and adjusting your mindset.

How to Overcome It: Reframe rejection as redirection. Imagine your life as a long hallway filled with doors. You knock on one (perhaps a romantic partner or a new job), and whoever answers thoroughly rejects you. They slam the door in your face.

While so many of us wind up standing there and wallowing in that sadness, the best way to move forward is simply to knock on another door. Maybe that person or opportunity wasn't meant to be because something much greater lies ahead behind a different door.

Why want something that doesn't want you?

Overcoming the fear of rejection means holding yourself to the highest standards so you can let go of opportunities that aren't for you.

Fear of Change

Change is indeed the only constant in life. Even the same routine repeated over and over will encounter minor changes daily. Psychologically speaking, a predictable routine satisfies our primal needs for comfort and familiarity. Predictability makes us feel safe.

Yet, many fear change because they feel out of control and out of their comfort zone. On a small scale, a fear of change can manifest as getting frustrated by unexpected changes or feeling overwhelmed by new job assignments outside your everyday responsibilities.

It may also show resistance to changing bad habits or developing new routines. The fear significantly worsens when enormous upheavals arise, such as a major breakup, moving to a new place, or trying to start a new business endeavour.

As you push back against change, it also pushes against you and tries to keep you stagnant. You may feel stubborn or blocked in trying to face your patterns and improve yourself. The fear of change ultimately prevents you from growing and evolving.

> *If you always do what you've always done, you'll always get what you've always got.*
>
> Henry Ford

We all have to face the fundamental truth: your reality can shift overnight or even in a single moment. One phone call. One conversation. One positive or negative event. That's all it takes!

Developing an adaptable attitude is essential to shielding you from the anxieties and stress of changing circumstances. Instead of resisting change, you can embrace it as part of your evolution.

How to Overcome It: Adaptability is the capacity to adjust to new conditions. It has allowed certain animal species to evolve while others have gone extinct. It's also one of the most coveted job skills among employers.

Fear of Public Speaking

Nearly 30% of Africans rank glossophobia (the fear of public speaking) as one of their biggest fears. Getting up in front of a crowd may awaken nightmare visions of people throwing tomatoes at you or "booing" every word you say.

While it may seem easy for "glossophobia" to avoid speaking in front of crowds, this fear can significantly hinder your success in the workplace and your social life. After all, public speaking isn't just something you do on stage at a TED Talk.

The Weight We Carry: A Blueprint for Dealing with Life's Burdens

Whether you're a high-achieving student, C-level executive, or small business owner, speaking is integral to everything from meetings to business pitches to dinner toasts. Finding comfort when speaking in front of a group of people can help you become more popular and a better leader.

How to Overcome It: Ultimately, the fear of speaking is rooted in the fear of criticism. Nobody wants to feel like their words, stories, or perspectives are being picked apart by an audience (whether that audience is 2 or 2,000). However, more often than not, your inner critic is the most ruthless of all.

Fear of Imperfection (or not being good enough)

Perfectionism is just a pretty mask for fear. It may look like perfectionists seek flawlessness because they hold such high standards for their work. But when you peek behind the curtain, people who claim perfectionism as a strength often struggle with:

Procrastination: The main problem with perfectionism is how it delays us from putting our work out into the world. If seeking the ultimate, unblemished final product, an artist could paint over little details indefinitely. You may do the same thing in your work projects, hobbies, or relationships.

Poor time management: If it takes an hour to write, edit, and re-read a simple email, you may have an issue with perfectionism. Because you badly want everything to be flawless, you waste a lot of time on things that may not matter in the long run.

Unreasonably high standards: Perfectionists tend to hold themselves to impossibly high standards and beat themselves up for minor setbacks.

How to Overcome It: If you have been putting off a particular project because it isn't perfect yet, this is the method for you. Whether it's developing a product, learning to paint, or creating social media content, try the "Throw Spaghetti at the Wall" Method and "see what sticks."

Stop overthinking and take imperfect action: You can always go back and make changes later. My first book, Success Comes in Seven Pieces, was published seven years ago and won three awards. My greatest fear when releasing this book was that it would be a one-hit wonder. I was afraid that the book would never be good enough. The proliferation of poorly planned TikTok and YouTube videos taught me that it does not always have to be perfect. You've probably seen a lot of poorly organised content on the internet, but it's working wonders. Set a goal of producing one or two imperfect videos per week if you want to start a YouTube channel. Look back at the first videos ever released by popular YouTubers to see how far they've progressed. While you can still strive to produce your best work, try to avoid striving for perfection at all costs.

> *Done is better than perfect.*
>
> Sheryl Sandberg

Set strict deadlines: One of the keys to overcoming perfectionism (especially in creative endeavours) is to start every project with a strict deadline for completion. This will help you focus on the largest, most important tasks instead of getting stuck on the details.

Toss ideas around and execute them instead of ruminating: Get a stack of index cards and make a "brain dump" stack. On each card, write down an idea you've been thinking about but not taking action on. Then shuffle the cards, grab one, and take action without hesitation.

Ask people you admire about their mistakes: When trying something new, it often seems like all the successful people in your field have it all figured out. They probably had to undergo much trial and error to get to where they were. Reach out to someone you admire and ask them about their biggest lessons from failures in their business, hobby, or career.

Fear of Vulnerability

In her book Daring Greatly, shame and vulnerability expert Brene Brown defines vulnerability as "uncertainty, risk, and emotional exposure." There is no denying that exposing your deeper emotions to friends, co-workers, or a significant other can be utterly terrifying.

But the caveat is that this fear can hold you back from major personal and professional opportunities. Science tells us that:

- Vulnerability improves employee motivation and connection with managers
- Vulnerability improves trust in leaders (especially when leaders are vulnerable enough to admit their shortcomings or mistakes)
- Self-disclosure can make others more likely to open up to you

- Vulnerability strengthens interpersonal relationships

Nonetheless, being open about your emotions or deepest fears is super hard. If you've been betrayed, shamed, or publicly embarrassed in the past, you've probably put up some walls to protect yourself emotionally.

This creates a paradox where:

- On the one hand, we are afraid of being lonely or without meaningful relationships.
- On the other hand, we are also scared to open up and be vulnerable because we might get hurt.

Vanessa Van Edwards calls this the "Relational Paradox" that can lead to a vicious cycle of unfulfilling relationships.

Fear of Time

Time anxiety or productivity shame is the feeling that "there's never enough time." Perhaps you feel rushed through life or like you can't get enough done in a day.

> *Time is what we want most, but what we use worst.*
>
> William Penn

But time is the one great equaliser: everyone has the same number of hours in a day, no matter their class, race, career, or location. Time is the one thing more valuable than any amount of money or a rare, precious jewel. It holds this value because, once it is gone, you can never get it back. That is understandably daunting.

However, the fear of not having enough time can cause undue anxiety and stress. Harvard's infamous happiness study found that people nearing the end of their lives regret working too much. Rushing through life is no way to live. You have to stop and smell the flowers! Plus, you need to be sure you're using your time to the best of your ability.

How to Overcome It: While a feeling of urgency can be great for the ultra-ambitious, it can also distract you from enjoying life in the present moment. Yes, time is passing with every tick of the clock. But you can take solace in knowing that life is long and you don't have to accomplish everything at this very moment. Instead:

Slow down and practice mindfulness: Mindfulness is simply being more present and aware of yourself as you perform daily tasks. It can help you slow down and realise that you have as much time as you need. Research shows that mindfulness meditation can significantly reduce anxiety and improve productivity. Try a daily meditation practice or a phone-free nature walk.

Monitor your screen time: Mindlessly checking your email or social media every 15 minutes can quickly eat up your most important hours of the day. Start monitoring your screen time or try a digital detox so you can focus on productivity in your own life instead of watching the lives of others. This alone will help you feel like you've magically created more time.

Improve time management: Little time-wasting habits can quickly devour your waking hours. Do you catch yourself multitasking and taking twice the necessary time to complete a project? Get a planner and start planning your day for the greatest productivity possible.

Use a productivity hack: Monitoring your rhythms or learning to speed read are little-known hacks for making your time work for you.

Fear of Loneliness

Humans are undeniably social animals with a need for companionship. Fear of loneliness is practically wired into our physiology. After all, ancient humans separated from their tribe were unlikely to survive.

However, without the risk of sabre tooth tigers or starvation, spending time alone in the modern day is scientifically proven to improve your health and well-being. Studies show that spending time in solitude is correlated with:

- Higher confidence
- More creativity
- Higher emotional intelligence
- More emotional stability in challenging situations

This is likely because alone time allows for deep reflection on yourself and your life. You can metaphorically clear the mirror of your mind to see yourself as you are rather than how others perceive you. If you fear aloneness, you may inadvertently become clingy or unsure of your identity in the absence of other people.

How to Overcome It: The best way to start valuing your alone time is to find something you genuinely enjoy and take yourself out on a date to do it. Get dressed up in your favourite outfit, head to a delicious restaurant or a place where you can do your favourite hobby, and enjoy the act of being you. Practice positive affirmations and celebrate a few things you love about yourself.

Caveat: However, if you feel chronically alone, it may be time to pick up a social hobby or take an inventory of your relationships to develop ways to feel less alone.

The key factor all these fears have in common is their sneaky tendency to sabotage our success.

In her inspiring TEDx Talk about overcoming your biggest fears, New York Times bestselling author Ruth Soukup describes why identifying and understanding your inner fears is so important. She asserts that every fear has two components:

- What is serving you
- What is holding you back

For example, a fear of vulnerability can serve you by protecting your heart from getting betrayed or hurt again after a terrible divorce. But it can also hold you back by preventing you from opening up and finding love again.

Similarly, a fear of imperfection may protect you from putting out sub-par work, but it can also hold you back from taking the action necessary to reach your goals.

Her insights help us remember that fear doesn't need to be embarrassing or shameful. It is part of your psyche for a reason.

Ultimately, analysing your fears from this perspective and using the action tips above can help you build the courage to face life's fears head-on.

Chapter Fourteen

Emotional Hygiene

Emotional hygiene is akin to the ecosystem of a pristine forest. In a forest, each component plays a vital role in maintaining balance, health, and sustainability. Similarly, emotional hygiene involves nurturing and preserving the delicate equilibrium of our inner emotional ecosystem.

Imagine your emotions as diverse species of plants and animals, and your mind as a lush forest. Just as different species coexist and rely on each other in an ecosystem, our emotions interconnect and influence one another within our minds. Emotional hygiene involves understanding and managing these interconnections to create harmony and well-being.

In a forest ecosystem, certain plants provide shelter and nourishment for animals, while animals aid in pollination and seed dispersal for plants. Similarly, positive emotions like joy, love, and gratitude act as nourishing plants, providing a nurturing environment for our minds. They attract positive experiences and deepen our connections with others.

Negative emotions, on the other hand, can be likened to harmful insects or invasive plant species that disrupt the ecosystem's balance. Just as invasive species can choke the growth of native plants, negative emotions can overshadow positive ones, leading to distress, anxiety, or depression. Emotional hygiene involves identifying and managing these negative emotions to prevent them from overpowering the positive aspects of our emotional ecosystem.

Like a forest undergoing natural disturbances such as storms or fires, we also encounter challenges and setbacks in life. Emotional hygiene prepares us to weather these storms by building resilience. It's like the deep root systems of trees that anchor them during strong winds, enabling them to stand tall. Through practices like self-care, self-reflection, and seeking support, we develop emotional resilience, allowing us to bounce back from difficulties and maintain our emotional well-being.

Just as a forest requires conservation and protection, emotional hygiene calls for the preservation and nurturing of our emotional ecosystem. We can cultivate emotional intelligence, mindfulness, and self-compassion, much like environmental stewardship preserves biodiversity. By valuing our emotional well-being and taking active steps to maintain it, we create an inner ecosystem that thrives with positivity, balance, and harmony.

Emotions are the most visible, pressing, and occasionally painful force in our lives. Every day, our emotions drive us. We take risks because we are excited about new opportunities. We cry when we are hurt, and we make sacrifices when we love. Without a doubt, our emotions have more power over our thoughts, intentions, and actions than our rational minds. However, when we act on our emotions too quickly or on the wrong kinds of emotions, we frequently make decisions that we later regret.

Our emotions can swing between dangerous extremes. You're on the verge of rage if you veer too far to the left. If you steer too far to the right, you will experience euphoria. Emotions, like many other aspects of life, are best addressed with moderation and a logical perspective. This is not to say that we should not fall in love or rejoice when we receive good news. These are the finer aspects of life. Negative emotions must be handled with extreme caution.

Negative emotions, such as rage, envy, or bitterness, have a tendency to spiral out of control, especially when they are triggered. These kinds of emotions can grow like weeds over time, slowly conditioning the mind to function on negative feelings and dominating daily life. Have you ever met someone who is consistently angry or hostile? They were not born in this manner. However, they allowed certain emotions to fester within them for so long that they became inbred feelings that surfaced all too frequently.

So, how can we avoid operating on the wrong types of feelings and master our emotions even in the most trying of situations?

I'm not sure, but all you need to do is find a way to clear your mind. Return to the first chapter and read about cleaning your mind. Maintain emotional hygiene at all costs.

Chapter Fifteen

We Often Regret Not Doing

Once upon a time, in the quaint village of Segwashi in GaMamabolo, nestled at the foot of the majestic Hwiti Mountain, eying the Drakensburg Mountains tailing into Haenertsburg valleys, there lived a young boy named Matome. Matome was known for his curiosity and adventurous spirit. He was always eager to explore the world around him, seeking new experiences and challenges.

One day, as Matome walked through the village square, he noticed a poster announcing auditions for a grand talent show. The auditions promised a chance to perform on a magnificent stage in front of a large audience. Excitement filled Matome's heart as he imagined showcasing his hidden talents and leaving the audience in awe.

However, doubts and insecurities soon crept into Matome's mind. He began to question his abilities and wondered if he was truly talented enough to stand out among the other performers. Fear of failure started to overshadow his initial enthusiasm, and he hesitated to sign up for the auditions.

The Weight We Carry: A Blueprint for Dealing with Life's Burdens

Days turned into weeks, and Matome continued to deliberate. He watched as his friends and fellow villagers eagerly prepared their acts, pouring their hearts and souls into their performances. The village buzzed with anticipation for the upcoming talent show.

As the final day for auditions approached, Matome found himself standing at a crossroads. He knew deep down that he had a unique gift to share with the world, but fear held him back from taking the leap. He pondered the possibilities, imagining the applause and recognition he could have received if only he had mustered the courage to participate.

The day of the talent show finally arrived. The village square transformed into a dazzling spectacle of lights, music, and laughter. The air was thick with anticipation and excitement. Matome stood on the outskirts, watching the performers take the stage one by one, each leaving a mark with their exceptional talents.

Regret slowly gnawed at Matome's heart. He realised that he had let fear dictate his choices, and now he was left with a sense of longing and what-ifs. The missed opportunity weighed heavily on him as he witnessed the fulfilment and joy that the other performers experienced.

From that day forward, Matome vowed to seize every opportunity that came his way. He promised himself that he would no longer allow fear to hold him back from pursuing his dreams. The experience served as a poignant reminder that inaction often leads to regret, and the only way to overcome it is to embrace courage and take the necessary steps towards our aspirations.

And so, Matome's story became a tale passed down through generations in the village, serving as a reminder to all who heard it that the only way to avoid the bitter taste of regret is to step forward, embrace opportunities, and wholeheartedly pursue our passions.

We have too many Matomes in our lives.

A study on "The temporal pattern of the experience of regret" found that more people regret things they didn't do than the things they did, even if the things they did turned out badly (Thomas & Husted, 1994). After all, with time and effort, you can fix almost any mistake, but you can't go back and do the things you dreamed of doing but didn't...which means you can only think about how today would be different if you had.

And now a new study by Gilovich and Davidai (2018) takes that idea even further, probing the kinds of regrets we have about the people we don't become, a natural extension of the actions we didn't take.

Researchers focused on three things:

- **Our actual selves:** the traits and abilities we think we possess; basically, who we think we are.
- **Our ought selves:** the traits and abilities we think we should possess; basically, who we think we should be (think responsibilities and obligations).
- **Our ideal selves:** the traits, abilities, and accomplishments we would like to possess; basically, our goals and hopes and dreams.

It makes sense that we regret not doing the things we think we are supposed to do: working harder at our professions, working harder to be healthier...it's natural to regret not working harder on things we ought to accomplish. But research shows most people (72 percent) feel regret related to their ideal selves as opposed to their ought selves (28 percent). In fact, when asked to name their single biggest life regret, 76 percent of participants cite an action not taken that would have helped them realise their ideal self.

That also makes sense. As one of the authors of the study says, "When we evaluate our lives, we think about whether we're heading towards our ideal selves, becoming the person we'd like to be. Those are the regrets that are going to stick with you because they are what you look at through the windshield of life.

"The 'ought' regrets are potholes on the road. Those were problems, but now they're behind you. To be sure, there are certain failures to live up to our 'ought' selves that are extremely painful and can haunt a person forever; so many great works of fiction draw upon precisely that fact.

"But for most people, those types of regrets are far outnumbered by the ways in which they fall short of their ideal selves."

In short, we most regret thinking we didn't reach our full potential. We most regret not becoming the person we feel we could have become...if we had only tried.

Because that is one mistake you can never go back and fix. But it is one mistake you can stop making today. To start taking action to realise your ideal self—to become the person you want to become—do the following:

1. Always make your goal tangible and specific

Assume you want to improve your fitness. "Get in better shape" sounds good, but what exactly does it mean? Nothing. It's only a wish.

"Lose 10 pounds in 30 days" is a specific, measurable, and attainable target. You not only know what you want to achieve, but setting that specific goal also allows you to create a process that will get you there.

You can plan your workouts and your diet...and then all you have to do is stick to it. I admire how Herbalife practitioners have mastered the art of goal-setting. They have what they call challenges that they must complete within a reasonable time frame. Thabo Madisha, a colleague, and his wife Nthabiseng transformed their bodies from overweight to sexy and healthy. Their programmes (challenges) are always time-bound and have a goal, such as growing biceps, leg work, ABS, shoulders, and so on.

Another example: "Grow my business" sounds good but has no meaning. "Land five new clients per month" lets you know exactly what you need to do to get those clients. Set a goal that allows you to work backward and design a process to achieve it. When you don't know what you want to achieve, it's impossible to know what to do every day. In event planning meetings, Victor Kgomoeswana, Executive Director of Marketing and Communication at the University of Limpopo, usually asks, "Could you please take me through the day of the event?" He requests that the organiser begin at the end, with a programme, getting into the venue, how it will look, and so on. It makes it much easier to plan a successful event, identify stakeholders, anticipate challenges, and prepare for them.

2. Always make your goal matter

If you want to get in better shape so other people will think you look better at the beach this summer, you're unlikely to follow through. Ultimately, who cares what other people think? (Your ideal self definitely shouldn't.) But if you want to get in better shape because you want to feel better and feel better about yourself, or to set an example for your kids, or to prove something to yourself...then you're much more likely to stick with it. Now your goal has meaning—not to your doctor, not to strangers on the beach, but to you.

That's true even if it's a silly goal, like when I did 10 000 push-ups in a year. You could say that's a meaningless goal, but I wanted to prove to myself that I could stick with something hard.

That goal meant something to me because it made a difference in how I saw myself, which made it a lot easier to stay the course.

3. Always make your goal a positive goal

"Stop criticising other people in meetings" is a great goal, but it's a negative goal. It's a lot harder to give up or stop doing something than it is to embrace a new and positive challenge.

Plus, setting a goal like "stop eating sweets" means you constantly have to choose to avoid temptation, and since willpower is often a finite resource (although there are ways to develop greater determination and willpower), why put yourself in a position of constantly needing to choose?

Always pick positive goals—that way you'll be working to become something new (and awesome) rather than to avoid being something you no longer wish to be.

4. Always set your goal, and then *forget* your goal

I know: We're told to focus on our goals.

Yet one of the biggest reasons people give up on huge goals is the distance between *here*, where you are today, and *there*, where you someday hope to be. If today you're able to run only a mile and your goal is to run a marathon, the distance between here and there seems insurmountable.

So you give up, because there's no way you'll get from here to there.

That's why almost all incredibly successful people set a goal and then focus all their attention on the process necessary to achieve that goal. Sure, the goal is still out there. But what they care about most is what they need to do today, and when they accomplish that, they feel happy about today. They feel good about today.

And they feel good about themselves because they've accomplished what they set out to do today. And that sense of accomplishment gives them all the motivation they need to do what they need to do when tomorrow comes—because success, even tiny, incremental success, is the best motivation of all.

When you savour the small victories, you get to feel good about yourself every day because you no longer feel compelled to compare the distance between here and there. You don't have to wait for "someday" to feel good about yourself; if you do what you planned to do today, you're a winner.

And that's why the most important step is to...

5. Always focus on the daily process

The Weight We Carry: A Blueprint for Dealing with Life's Burdens

The key to long-term success is to create a process that guarantees a series of small improvements. Usually, that means that what you do won't be that different from what other successful people do.

Along the way, you might make small corrections as you learn what works best for you, but never start by doing what you *want* to do, what *feels* good, or what you *think* might work.

Do what is proven to work. Otherwise, you'll give up because the process you create won't yield those small successes that keep you motivated and feeling good about yourself.

Which, if you think about it, is the perfect definition of success. And is the perfect way to avoid the regret of not becoming your ideal self.

Chapter Sixteen

Pressures of Life

The pressures of life are like the weight of a heavy backpack on a long hike. Imagine embarking on a challenging hike, carrying a backpack filled with supplies and equipment. At the beginning, the backpack feels manageable, but as you venture further, the weight begins to take its toll.

Similarly, the pressures of life accumulate as you progress on your journey. The backpack represents the responsibilities, expectations, and obligations that you carry on your shoulders. It includes work-related stress, personal relationships, financial burdens, and societal expectations. Initially, you may feel capable of managing it all, but as time goes on, the weight becomes increasingly burdensome.

Just as a heavy backpack can slow you down, the pressures of life can make you feel weighed down and overwhelmed. The weight may hinder your progress, exhaust your energy, and make each step more challenging. It's easy to lose sight of the beauty around you and become focused solely on the weight you're carrying.

The Weight We Carry: A Blueprint for Dealing with Life's Burdens

In one way or another, a large proportion of young people are subjected to insurmountable life pressures. Young people are dealing with hundreds of issues at once, rather than just one.

Under these economic conditions, mental illness among young people in the workplace is woefully under-addressed. With retrenchments, harsher working conditions, and uncertainty plaguing the minds of South Africa's shrinking and ageing workforce, young, employed people risk lower levels of productivity because life for the average worker is decidedly tougher. Higher living costs as a result of consecutive fuel and food price increases this year have put a tremendous strain on the country's breadwinners and young entry-level workers.

Young people congregate in large numbers to drink, but there aren't nearly as many gatherings for the purpose of uplifting themselves and their communities. This demonstrates the significant gap that exists between leadership and youth-focused community development. Young people are desperate for hope. They lack vision and a guiding hand to show them how to thrive. Unfortunately, government and community-based organisations' efforts to create productive and safe communities in which young people can thrive are not reaching everyone quickly enough. To combat this growing social crisis, we need the support of all stakeholders.

The crisis is exacerbated by young people entering the labour force—perhaps those fortunate enough to be 22 years old. We have young people with entry-level salaries living large because of our country's low financial literacy levels and social pressures among this age group. Here are a few pressures that are both necessary and not, depending on one's state of mind.

Moses Moreroa

Living Large

If the financial sector is good at one thing, it is creating millions of people who are creditworthy but not wealthy. Someone who starts a job with a salary of R20 000 feels obligated to own a luxury car.

To avoid mentioning brand names, there is a popular small car that costs around half a million with expensive insurance and installment. Someone with an R25 000 gross salary ends up living like a middle-class person, despite the fact that they are extremely poor. They live hand-to-mouth, and if their employer does not pay them on a monthly basis, they are homeless like someone who has never worked in his or her life. The car will be repossessed, the landlord will evict them, they will go hungry, and they will not have enough money to print new CVs.

Nobody but the system is to blame for this. The system is cruel and does not require an egotistical, unconscious spender. The system does not require a materialistic individual; it devours mercilessly. Let us examine the basic income and expenditures of someone earning R25 000 per month.

How much you need to earn to be middle class in South Africa

According to BusinessTech article published in July 2023, If one was to look at the average salary in South Africa across the formal sector as a metric of the middle class, Stats SA data shows that currently, it is R25 304 per month. The latest figures from the statistics agency's quarterly employment survey showed a 2.7% decrease from the final quarter of 2022, which was roughly R26 000.

The new average salary is, however, 6.8% up from the first quarter of 2022 R23 697. Multiple sources regard an income of just above R20

000 as middle class. For example, the University of Cape Town's Liberty Institute of Strategic Marketing argues that those earning roughly R22 000 makes a household middle class. Now, in the following page, let us look at what a middle class in South Africa goes through. They start a year with a zero balance in January, calling it Jan *wa wara*, meaning one hassles for money to return to work.

YOUR INCOME/EXPENDITURE

Income Statement

	2023 current year	2022 prior year
INCOME		
Gross Salary	R25 000,00	
Total Gross	**R25 000,00**	**R0,00**
EXPENSES		
Rent/Lease	R3 500,00	-
Grocery	R2 000,00	-
Vehicle Finance	R5 500,00	-
Vehicle Insurance	R1 800,00	-
Fuel	R1 500,00	-
Office Lunch	R800,00	-
Entertainment	R1 500,00	-
Girlfriend Allowance	R1 000,00	-
PAYE	R6 250,00	-

Telephone Expenses (Phone + Data)	R900,00	—
TOTAL EXPENSES	R24 750,00	R0,00
NET/TAKE HOME	R250,00	R0,00

I did not include clothing installments and furniture in this income/expenditure table, assuming they were purchased in cash, which is highly unlikely. I just don't want to add to your misery. But if that is the case, the installments have not been paid. If you were to search their phones for Fabiani, Truworths, Markham's, etc., you'd find, "Hi Mr Moreroa, note your Fabiani account is overdue. Please pay R2300 immediately to save further interest charges or avoid your account being handed over." Those who know me know that I cannot afford Fabiani. This is just an example.

Young people have no money to save after they are paid. Now that they are wearing expensive clothes, some of which are designer, the R250 that remains after key expenses have been met cannot sustain them.

They reversed some debit orders, that's what. The first casualty of a debit order is vehicle insurance. Hmmm! Money In+ of at least R1800. Do not expect them to pay off the clothing account; shortfalls are acceptable. In that regard, they are blacklisted. Anyway, their credit score is no longer relevant because they already own a car. Retail outlets can go to hell. The money is spent on groove, and the majority of these young people are involved in multiple romantic relationships. This is more financing. The other girlfriend(s) are covered by the R1800 reverse vehicle insurance.

The Weight We Carry: A Blueprint for Dealing with Life's Burdens

Here is a girlfriend's maintenance: the main chick received R1000. She understands because she lives with him and is aware of his difficulties. So, as long as she has her hair and nails done and they have a good time, life is good – *na enjoyment*. The following is the total cost of hosting a girl.

Side-Chick Chronicles	2023 current year
Revenue	
START	R1 800,00
Total Funds	**R1 800,00**
Expenses	
Pizza	R180,00
Soft Drink	R25,00
Ice Cream	R30,00
Dinner	R150,00
Alcohol	R300,00
Mavuso (take home)	R500,00
Data	R150,00

Total Expenses	R1 335,00
Net	R465,00

Only about R500 remains from the reversed vehicle insurance, and this is only a day after the debit reversal. You can envision the next 20 days. This cost is only for a basic girl, not for those with frontals who drink shots and dine at expensive restaurants. I'm not referring to those who drink the cider from a long bottle.

Oh! Boy, boy! The stress is simply too much. I'm referring to a young man who doesn't send anything home and comes from a low-income family. I'm referring to a young man who is childless. Imagine having a child while the nation is fatherless.

This person is already bankrupt. They reverse the vehicle insurance every month, and the insurer automatically cancels the insurance after two months. What they are thinking is that an accident will not happen to them. He drives carefully on the roads, aware of what he has done, but an accident is about more than just you. You can drive well and still get hit.

If a motorist does not have insurance and their car is involved in an accident, it can be financially ruinous. Unfortunately, most drivers are unaware of the high costs of repairing an accident-damaged vehicle.

When this occurs, most uninsured motorists will attempt to self-repair their vehicles, resulting in cars with minor repairs that are no longer roadworthy. This puts even more strain on our roads in terms of accidents, and it also puts many innocent motorists at risk due to this type of negligence.

A car may be written off, depending on the severity of the accident. Imagine having to cover the cost of a new car if you caused the accident and don't have insurance, or worse, if someone is seriously injured and you have to cover those costs as well. Most people will be bankrupt as a result of this.

Given the likelihood of an accident, motorists should at the very least consider third-party insurance, as the cost of an accident is far greater than a monthly installment.

Let's say someone is in a minor accident and repairs themselves. With how much money? They can't live without a car, so will they have to walk again? *Aneva*! As a result, the young man will borrow money from friends in order to repair the car. How will he pay off his debt? Unlikely. Friendships are ruined, and the person borrows from one friend to the next until they have no choice but to go to a bank to borrow.

They become deeply in debt and begin to reverse the vehicle installment. The bank will give him a reprieve the first time and make plans to pay off the arrears the following month. The young man then fails to honour the agreement, and the bank charges interest on the arrears. The bank repossesses the car after the third default on repayment.

The bank will auction the car after repossessing it. The auction is terminated when the car's market value is reached at the time of reselling. After two to three years, that R500 000 car is now worth R80 000, and the young man's remaining repayment is around R180 000. This means that if the auction is successful, the car will be purchased for R80 000, with the remaining debt on the vehicle being

R100 000. Unfortunately, even after repossession, the young man still owes the bank R100 000.

Eish! This is because the young man did not even purchase short-fall insurance, which would have assisted in settling the R100 000. He wouldn't because it would be too expensive. Besides, he doesn't even have a life insurance policy or a funeral plan—I'm sure you figured that out from the income-expenses table. And his employer does not even deduct medical aid. He begins to experience stress, becomes depressed, and, without medical assistance, - ke mathata. He begins to miss work, goes AWOL, loses focus, underperforms, and is fired. 'Jisas'!

It is not witchcraft, but rather life's pressures. Imagine if the car was in a serious accident and was written off without insurance, and you ended up paying for a car that is no longer alive and well. Nothing is better now that the repossessions are gone. It's a Catch-22 situation.

Will the main chick and the side chicks stick by him now? Following his eviction from his flat? His levels of depression will sink him. He must now return home—to what? He only built three rooms, and they live in an RDP with a family of four. What would the community think if they knew he lived as if he had everything? I'm pretty sure he's not going home.

The rest, as they say, is history!

I wish we could learn the art of saving for investment rather than rainy days. It is possible to become a millionaire before the age of 30 if you start working at the age of 22 and earn R25 000 per month. If

The Weight We Carry: A Blueprint for Dealing with Life's Burdens

you save R10 000 per month for 30 years, you will have R960 000 saved. The monthly difference could be R15 000.

The R960 000 could be put to good use as an investment, with the money working for them to generate multiple streams of income. We must master the art of diversifying and amplifying our talents. If you enjoy the groove, you could own your joint and become a VIP at your lifestyle centre in just eight years. Let us not rush into a life of luxury; it is costly and difficult to maintain. It affects not only the wallet but also the mind, body, and soul. Living recklessly is a disaster in and of itself—a regrettable misfortune.

If you are paying rent next to your workplace, is there an urgent need for a car? I am starting to ask upsetting questions. I know you are pressured to show off that "*dilo di chentsitse*" but I am not sure if "*dithapelo tla be di landile*" or your ego is setting you up for a state of emergency.

I understand you can't be "*ba straata*" on your feet. You need a panoramic sunroof and dope rims. I understand, but the pressure will be your undoing. You will explode before you realise your full potential. Your dream life will never come true in your early twenties; that is a fantasy. You have the illusion of power. Your early years should be spent earning, not spending.

The mindset distinguishes poor, middle-class, and wealthy people. They all begin with a blank slate. According to one wise man in a masterclass, the difference is not how much money they make or even how much money they have. The difference between rich, middle-class, and poor people is their perception of the purpose of money.

Poor people believe that money's primary purpose is to pay bills. So the only reason they go to work every day is to get some money at the end of the month and give it to someone else.

The middle class believes that the primary purpose of money is to build credit so that they can buy things they can't afford and pay them off over time.

Rich people understand that the primary purpose of money is to multiply it. They take the money they earn, turn it into more money, and only then do they become wealthy. They understand that the only way to become wealthy is to keep the money for an extended period of time. They invested the funds in a maternity ward.

You will lose whatever you mismanage. The comfort zone is one of the greatest enemies of success and growth. You become accustomed to spending your money in the same manner and look forward to the day when you will receive it again and spend it. You don't want to change and will fight any growth plan that comes your way. When people are under pressure, they usually find a million reasons not to change.

Learned helplessness is another enemy of financial freedom. This is where a person feels they can't do things any other way than the way society expects them to.

The third foe that puts us under pressure is the path of least resistance. One is always looking for the simplest way to achieve a goal. But nothing worthwhile comes easily.

Like Charlie Munger puts it, it is not resisting the pressures of life and saving up money that is important in this regard; it is the person that you must become in order to resist the pressures of life. You have to

The Weight We Carry: A Blueprint for Dealing with Life's Burdens

become a completely different person. You have to develop character beyond that of 99% of the people in the world. You have to be honest, disciplined, and build quality relationships. Also, the willingness to work and set priorities is important, because without that, nothing is possible. So, once you reach your first savings target, you are a person who rose above the pressures of life, and you can now have more. You've got to work harder on yourself than you work on your job. If you work hard at your job, you can make a living. If you work hard on yourself, you can make a fortune.

Life is basically not what happens to you but what you do. Do today what will save you tomorrow. You should not be afraid of taking the risk of defying societal norms of spending and showing off to pursue something meaningful. You should not be afraid of your peers thinking you are poor and less progressive. You should be more afraid of falling into the pressures of life and remaining in the same miserable place. The clock is ticking, and if you are miserable now (living on a hand-to-mouth basis) and change nothing for the next five years, you will be much more miserable. By then, you will be a lot older to do what you could have done, and the same society will mock you for having blown it all away.

Stop trying to please people. You are under no obligation to set yourself on fire to keep everyone warm. Life can be heavy, especially when you want to carry it all at once. The more you fear something, the more it will happen; the pressure you are under will definitely crash you.

Let me leave you with two things you should never do in your life until you are rich:

- **Do not buy a lifestyle.** Buy assets first then you get a lifestyle.

- **Don't get into big debt and then burn your credit score.** The score is like your social security number. Live a debt-free life.

Chapter Seventeen

Distracted & Destroyed

Distractions are like a swarm of buzzing bees on a sunny day. Picture yourself sitting outside, trying to enjoy the warmth and tranquilly, when suddenly a group of bees comes buzzing around you. They fly erratically, creating a constant hum that captures your attention and disrupts your peaceful state. You find yourself swatting at them, trying to shoo them away, but they persistently distract you from your original intention of relaxation. Just as the bees divert your focus and make it difficult to enjoy the moment, distractions in life can swarm around us, making it challenging to concentrate on what truly matters. Like a skilled beekeeper, we must learn to navigate through the distractions, protecting our focus and maintaining our productivity amidst the buzzing chaos.

In my not-so-long life, I have witnessed strong men tumble down, to whom I grew admiration. Their fate is almost similar: they got distracted and allowed the enemy to get inside information, which destroyed them. What are your strengths? How do you use them?

The story of Samson in the Bible succinctly catches my point: when you make strides and operate in your gifts, you are bound to stand out, and there are so many people who wish to have the same. We may make plenty of physical results, but we all operate in a higher power that gives and sustains our wisdom. That is a special fuel to propel us forward and cannot be transferred or shared with others.

Samson made a covenant with God, and his mission would require physical strength. The Lord made a covenant with Samson that as long as he obeyed the Lord, he would be physically strong. Samson's long hair (see Judges 13:5) was a sign of this covenant.

When Samson kept his covenants, he was blessed with the ability to help his people, but when he broke his covenants, he lost both his spiritual and physical strength.

But Samson was distracted and destroyed. Samson had a woman problem. He survived a thousand men, but he could not survive a woman. The reason he was in Gaza previously was to be with a prostitute. Later, he was in the Valley of Sorek with Delilah, who was not his wife. Delilah was a Philistine. The leaders of the land each promised to pay her 1100 pieces of silver for her help in discovering Samson's strength and for bringing him into captivity.

There are people who come to you disguised as friends, but their interaction with you is always probing. They always ask personal questions about your family, your children, your cars, your work, etc. They want to know how much you have, how much you spend, and your source of survival. What do they want to use the information for?

Through various attempts and pleadings, which you can read about in the story of Samson and Delilah, she was able to uncover his weakness. Samson was taken prisoner with the help of Delilah.

Someone who is searching you out is unrelenting. Samson's hair had been cut, and his eyes had been gouged out. He was taken to the grinding wheel of the Philistines. Samson was publicly humiliated. How many of your friends do you drink with, party with, and trust with your life? What do they say when you begin to be poor and unable to provide for your family? Do they praise you for at least enjoying life and taking care of them? Most of them actually supply you with drugs, boyfriends or girlfriends, and anything else that has the potential to distract you from your purpose in life. They are the first to check up on you and tell the world what a loser you have become.

The main thing is to humiliate you. Every talented man or woman can quickly be destroyed by assassinating their character. Your success comes from your aura, your high standards, your ethics, and your reputation. I don't believe Samson's strength was wrapped up in the length of his hair. His strength was something that was given to him by God for a purpose. We see that the Spirit of God moved upon Samson to give him his strength (Judges 14:6). When Samson continually disregarded the vow, or calling, that God bestowed upon him, that is when his strength was taken away from him.

We had uprising football stars whose careers were cut short through character killing. If you appear in the news as a drunkard, will your team make you a candidate? How many videos of celebrities surfaced with them doing mischievous stuff? Who took the videos, as most of them are in private spaces? What was the purpose of taking it and uploading it for the world to see?

In the same way, Samson was placed in front of the prison house to be humiliated once again. He asked the young boy who led him out (presumably like a dog on a leash) to place his hands on the pillars of the building.

Though blinded and humiliated—or maybe because he was finally humbled—Samson prayed that God would allow him to do a work on behalf of Israel once again. God granted him the strength to knock down the building. The Bible says that Samson slew more in his death under the rubble of the building than he did in his life.

It shows that when we maintain discipline and focus, we are bound to achieve more. Hard work and discipline beat talent. Most talented people get well over themselves and want to have it all their way. There are always regulations in any area of operation. No matter how talented you are, you need to remain within the confines of your operation.

Though Samson accomplished the purposes of God, I often wonder how much more powerful and effective he would have been had he also honoured God with his life.

Lessons to Learn

- God often works in spite of our rebellion.
- God allows us to make wrong choices. He will not force us to follow and obey Him.
- Though God does not force us to obey, He can withhold His blessings and empowerment when we don't.
- Though God did not visit your parents or my parents with a set of instructions for us before we were born, He has given us His Word that should guide us in our daily lives.

The Weight We Carry: A Blueprint for Dealing with Life's Burdens

Similarly, when we become distracted in the spaces in which we operate—whether at work, school, in relationships, etc.—we are easily destroyed. When we become overconfident in our abilities, we undermine the sources of our power.

The first effect of distractions is to blur our vision, just as Samson's eyes were extorted. He became aimless because he couldn't see where he was going.

Distractions catch us like a lion on the hunt. A bite to the neck or throat kills the animal quickly. Lions approach larger prey from an angle, jumping on top and using their own weight to wrestle the animal to the ground, biting at the vertebrae in an attempt to sever the spinal cord.

Distractions are an effective weapon. They strike where it hurts the most and target areas that are beyond repair. Most marriages end because one of the partners becomes distracted and makes a critical error that cannot be repaired. Even if one partner forgives, the damage is irreversible and serves as a constant reminder that the person cannot be trusted with the responsibility of leading the family. When people get involved with married men or women, they often act as if they don't mind or even enjoy the situation. The goal is to weaken the cheating partner and take control.

Because someone is talented, their greatest weakness, like a lion, is their selfishness. They are only concerned with themselves and put themselves forward in all situations. When you are overwhelmed by your abilities and success, you display your strengths.

Anything that seeks to destroy you will first study your vision, deprive you of your power, and mislead you. To destroy Samson, the Philistines cut off his hair (power), removed his eyes (vision), and led him to a rock (direction), where he became disoriented. The Philistines did not kill Samson; he asked to die with them.

They start your demise, make you believe you have nothing to live for, and then let you finish it. They draft the contract, which you sign. Don't approve other people's plans.

Refuse to go to places that do not match your skills. Say no to anything that could harm your reputation. Refuse invitations that cast doubt on your intentions. Refuse to plan for any game whose strategy you do not understand. You will be destroyed if you are distracted.

Chapter Eighteen

Solute or Solvent Friends?

Once upon a time, in Segwashi village—those who know it love how it is nestled amidst the rolling hills of Spitzkop, Houtbosdorp, and Veekraal, apportioned by the valleys and rivers of Monare and Mphogodiba—there lived a young dreamer named Motume. Motume was known for his inquisitive mind and his knack for making decisions. He believed that life's choices were akin to solubility, where the right decisions dissolved the challenges that lay ahead.

Motume had a quest to find his true passion in life. He embarked on a journey, carrying a flask that symbolised his decision-making ability. Inside the flask, he carried different solutes, each representing a different path he could take.

As Motume traversed through the forests of the Lebowa Government and crossed the Mphogodiba and Monare Rivers, he encountered various people who shared their stories and wisdom. They became like solvents, ready to interact with his choices and guide him towards the right path.

The first person he met was a kind and patient mentor named Wisdoma. She represented the solvent of experience. Wisdoma shared tales of her own life, providing valuable insights and lessons. As Motume listened, he noticed that her stories dissolved his doubts and fears, making his decision-making process clearer.

Next, Motume met a daring adventurer named Courageus, whose father owned a nursery plantation called Kromdraai Blomme. He embodied the solvent of bravery. Courageus inspired Motume to take risks and step out of his comfort zone. Each time Motume poured the solvent of courage into his flask, it dissolved his hesitation, making him bolder in pursuing his passions.

On his journey, Motume encountered a compassionate artist named Empathya How I wish she featured Motlanalo in one of her soulful songs. She symbolised the solvent of understanding. Empathya had a unique ability to dissolve barriers of judgement and prejudice. As Motume conversed with her, he noticed how her understanding dissolved his confusion, allowing him to see the world from different perspectives.

As Motume continued his quest, he met a wise elder named Patienceus, the embodiment of the solvent of patience. Patienceus taught him the art of waiting and reflecting. Whenever Motume encountered a challenging decision, he would add a few drops of patience to his flask. It dissolved his impatience, enabling him to make decisions with a clear and calm mind.

Throughout his journey, Motume faced moments of uncertainty and doubt. However, he understood that just as solutes dissolve in solvents, his choices could dissolve obstacles and lead him to his true passion.

The Weight We Carry: A Blueprint for Dealing with Life's Burdens

With his flask of solvents in hand, Motume finally arrived at a serene mountaintop in the Debengeni Falls, overlooking a breath-taking valley. He took a deep breath and pondered over his experiences and the solvents that had guided him.

As Motume looked down at the valley, he realised that the choices he had made had dissolved his fears, insecurities, and uncertainties. He had found his true passion—helping others through his creativity and empathy.

Motume's story reminds us that in life, decision-making is like solubility. The right choices, guided by wisdom, courage, empathy, and patience, can dissolve our doubts, fears, and obstacles, leading us to a fulfilling and purposeful life.

And so, with his newfound clarity and understanding, Motume descended from the Debengeni mountaintop, ready to embrace his passion and continue his journey, knowing that solubility, both in chemistry and in life, held the power to transform and guide him towards a meaningful future.

I know I sound like a scientist, but believe me when I say I've never been in a science lecture. Lethabo Hlahla, who frequently uses scientific terms in our conversations, has piqued my interest in learning more about science and how it constructs reality. Now, to avoid confusing my general stream friends, let's talk about solubility and compare it to a puzzle.

Solubility is like a puzzle piece fitting into a larger picture. Imagine you have a collection of puzzle pieces, each with a unique shape and design. Some pieces easily fit together, seamlessly joining to form a complete picture, while others resist integration and remain separate. Solubility works in a similar way.

Substances, like puzzle pieces, have their own characteristics that determine their ability to dissolve in a particular solvent. Just as puzzle pieces fit together based on their shapes and interlocking mechanisms, solutes dissolve in solvents when their molecular structures and interactions are compatible. If the solute's properties are compatible with the solvent's, they intermingle, creating a homogeneous solution. However, if the solute and solvent are incompatible, they remain distinct, like two mismatched puzzle pieces that won't connect. Solubility, therefore, can be seen as the compatibility between the solute and solvent, determining whether they merge harmoniously or remain separate entities.

What kind of friends come into your life? We know some come for a reason, some for a season, and others for a lifetime. That is okay; it will always be the case. A major concern now is the effect these people have on your life, whether they came for a season, reason, or lifetime. What kind of solutions do these people pour into your life? Whether good or bad, there's always a solution they will bring; they may bring the right solution to your problem or a problem to your solutions.

Let me give an example of an interesting chemical interaction between substances. Perhaps defining the concepts in the title will set the context. When one substance dissolves into another, a solution is formed. A solution is a homogeneous mixture consisting of a solute dissolved in a solvent. The *solute* is the substance that is being dissolved, while the *solvent* is the dissolving medium. Solutions can be formed with many different types and forms of solutes and solvents.

From what I can tell, I want us to ignore the taste and concentrate on what we see. When orange juice is poured into water, it destroys it; it dominates.

The Weight We Carry: A Blueprint for Dealing with Life's Burdens

However, salt is destroyed by being thrown into water, whereas water and oil do not mix at all, so there is no destroying; there is no solution.

Let's look at who comes into your life—the type of friends you have, the impact you or they have on you, and whether or not there is any impact at all. In times of need, it is not so much about who you know as it is about who you have.

We frequently value and prioritise those who come to us to dilute our potential because their goal is to question our intentions and make us feel and appear to be heading in the wrong direction. They give us the impression that we are losing touch with reality because we are overly ambitious. For example, suppose you are a born-again Christian with aspirations to serve the Lord and grow in spirit, but your friend is a womaniser, drinks alcohol, parties, and constantly tells you about everything that has the potential to taint your faith and reputation.

What kind of solution does he propose for your life? What would people think of you if you hung out with people who had opposing personalities? Does it improve or harm your character? Is there a way to make your dream come true? If you want a good solution, stop combining the wrong substances. Stop bringing solvents into your life if you want your dream to come true; it will be dissolved.

At work, the same thing occurs. There are people who exist solely to dissolve any initiatives or projects (solute) simply because they are not in charge of the process. They spread negativity through deception, sabotage, and hatred. The solution they seek is for the projects to be dissolved. If you are young and want to grow, surround yourself with people who will help you grow in your life, sharpen your critical thinking, and help you ascend to the next rung on your career ladder.

Some people see potential in you and want to sell you a conspiracy to make you doubt yourself and the people you should be mixing with. You begin to dislike those who will assist you in growing in favour of those who are afraid of your potential. As solvents, such colleagues will dilute a leader's vision, dissolve your hopes in the organisation, and leave you befuddled. That is their solution: to render you inactive (dissolved). They will go to great lengths to deceive you into believing that you are being taken advantage of, that you are being overlooked, that you are better than the master, that you can be independent and do not need to work in a team, and so on. With just one mistake in mixing with such people, your potential is squandered.

Normally, a car-owning friend becomes the favourite. You're being fuelled to go out every now and then, drink and drive, and hang out with all the bad guys. Mixing with such a crowd will result in accidents, traffic tickets, punctures, high kilometres, worn-out tyres, and so on, all of which will reduce the value of your car and increase maintenance patterns. What is the solution? Your possessions will dissolve.

Chapter Nineteen

Activity Without Productivity

Activity without productivity is like running on a treadmill without actually going anywhere. Imagine stepping onto a treadmill, setting it at a high speed, and vigorously running in place. You exert energy, sweat, and even feel a sense of accomplishment from your physical activity. However, despite all the effort, you remain in the same spot, never making any progress towards your destination. In this scenario, your actions are characterised by a lot of movement, but ultimately they lack purpose and tangible results. Similarly, engaging in tasks or actions without a clear goal or meaningful outcome can leave you feeling busy but unproductive. It's important to ensure that your efforts are directed towards meaningful objectives so you can make progress and achieve desired results instead of simply spinning your wheels.

Chapter Twenty

Hasta La Vista

"Hasta la vista" is a Spanish phrase that translates to "Until we see each other again" in English. It became popularised by the movie "Terminator 2: Judgement Day," where Arnold Schwarzenegger's character, the Terminator, famously says "Hasta la vista, baby" before delivering a line or taking action. It has since been used as a catchphrase to bid farewell or indicate that a separation or departure is temporary. So, if you're using "Hasta la vista" as a way to say goodbye, it implies that you expect to meet or see the person again in the future.

Whenever I remember these words, I relate them to the reality of life. Sometimes you must step away in order to return with greater strength, resilience and perspective. Just not Ricky Rick's way, please. It's like taking a break from a challenging workout to allow your muscles to recover and rebuild, ultimately enabling you to push harder and achieve better results in the long run. Similarly, in life, there are moments when it's necessary to temporarily distance yourself from a situation, a relationship, or a particular environment to gain clarity, recharge and grow. This period of absence allows you to reflect, learn valuable lessons, and develop new skills or perspectives.

When you eventually come back, you do so with renewed energy, enhanced wisdom, and the ability to approach challenges with a fresh mindset. Just as a phoenix rises from the ashes, leaving and returning stronger can be a transformative experience that propels you to new heights of personal growth and success.

Do not be afraid to step aside and pick a side that will work. You can come back later. Let me give you an example of how it feels to start afresh. Imagine you're an artist with a fresh canvas in front of you. It's empty, devoid of any strokes or colours. You may feel a mixture of excitement and uncertainty, but deep down, you know that this blank slate holds endless possibilities. Similarly, in life, there are moments when starting over can be intimidating. Whether it's changing careers, beginning a new relationship, or pursuing a different path, fear of the unknown may try to hold you back. However, just like the artist who takes a brush and starts creating, you have the power to embrace the blank canvas of opportunity. It's an invitation to explore new passions, discover hidden talents, and rewrite your story. Embracing the chance to start again allows you to learn from past experiences, grow from challenges, and design a future that aligns with your true desires. So, don't be afraid to begin anew, for it is in those moments that you can create something beautiful and uniquely yours.

So, Hasta la Vista, baby!

Chapter Twenty-One

Afraid Of Being Afraid

Imagine you're standing on the edge of a diving board, about to jump into a swimming pool. You feel a surge of fear and anxiety about taking the leap. However, in addition to this initial fear, you also start to become afraid of your own fear. You worry about what will happen if you let fear control you, and this secondary fear starts to hold you back even more.

The diving board represents a situation or trigger that induces fear. The first fear you experience is your natural response to the potential risks or uncertainties associated with the situation. However, the fear of being afraid adds an additional layer of anxiety and can prevent you from taking action or facing the situation.

In order to overcome this cycle of fear, it's important to address both levels of fear separately. You can work on managing the initial fear by understanding its causes, gradually exposing yourself to the situation, and seeking support. Simultaneously, you can work on the fear of being afraid by recognising that it's normal to feel fear and learning to accept and manage it without letting it control your actions.

Just as you can learn to take the leap off the diving board by managing your fears, you can also learn to face and overcome your fears in other areas of life. By breaking down fear into manageable parts and building your resilience, you can gradually reduce the fear of being afraid and gain the confidence to navigate challenging situations with greater ease.

In short, deal with fear as it comes, or else fear will give birth to another fear, and you will fear the fact that you are fearing when you shouldn't.

Chapter Twenty-Two

Close The Cracks

I like imaginations because they can take you to places you never thought existed. Imagine you are the owner of a house that has been standing for many years. Over time, you start to notice small cracks forming in the walls, gaps in the doors and windows, and leaks in the roof. These imperfections represent the vulnerabilities and weaknesses in different aspects of your life.

To address these issues, you decide to embark on a renovation project. You hire contractors and craftsmen to fix the cracks, seal the gaps, and repair the leaks. They diligently work to strengthen the structure and make it more secure, ensuring that no further damage will occur.

The house symbolises your life, and the cracks and gaps represent areas of vulnerability or inefficiency. The renovation project represents the proactive steps you take to address and improve these areas. By closing the cracks, you reinforce the foundation of your life, enhancing its stability and making it more resilient.

Just as renovating a house requires identifying the weak spots and actively working to repair them, closing the cracks in life involves recognising the areas that need improvement and taking action to strengthen them. It's about actively engaging in personal growth, self-reflection, and making positive changes to enhance various aspects of your life, just as you would renovate and repair a house to make it better.

"To close the cracks in life" is not an established idiom or phrase, but it can be interpreted as a metaphorical expression meaning to address or fix the weaknesses, gaps, or problems that exist in various aspects of one's life. It suggests taking action to mend or strengthen areas that may have been neglected or overlooked.

In this context, "cracks" represent areas of vulnerability or inefficiency that can hinder personal growth, happiness, or success. It could refer to different aspects of life, such as relationships, career, health, personal development, or overall well-being.

Closing the cracks in life involves recognising and actively working on improving those areas. It may involve self-reflection, setting goals, making positive changes, seeking support or guidance, and taking steps to address any shortcomings or challenges. It's about being proactive in creating a more fulfilling and balanced life.

For example, if someone feels that their relationships lack depth or emotional connection, they might focus on improving their communication skills or investing more time and effort in building stronger connections with loved ones.

In terms of career, it could involve identifying and addressing any skill gaps, seeking professional development opportunities, or re-evaluating career choices to align better with personal goals.

Ultimately, "closing the cracks in life" implies a proactive approach to self-improvement and taking responsibility for making positive changes in areas that need attention or enhancement.

Chapter Twenty-Three

Sowing Discord In Fields Of Peace

In the vast landscape of relationships, there are individuals who, like the disruptive wind, take pleasure in breaking the bonds that connect people. In my village, there is a young lady named Malehufa who finds satisfaction in creating divisions and dismantling relationships.

Just as some people revel in chaos, Malehufa thrives on the fragmentation of connections. People like her derive a sense of power and control from sowing discord and severing the ties that bind people together.

Malehufa sees relationships as fragile structures, ripe for manipulation and destruction. She may exploit vulnerabilities, exploit misunderstandings, or instigate conflicts to create rifts between friends, families, or partners.

For Malehufa, breaking relationships provides a sense of gratification. She finds pleasure in the emotional turmoil that ensues, or has personal motives, such as seeking revenge or gaining a sense of superiority over others.

In their wake, the Malehufas of this world leave a trail of broken trust, hurt feelings, and fractured bonds. Like a destructive force, they disrupt the harmony and mutual understanding that once existed, leaving a void in the lives of those affected.

However, it is essential to recognise that the actions of such people stem from their own insecurities, unresolved conflicts, or a deep-rooted desire to exert control over others. Their enjoyment of breaking relationships often masks their own emotional pain and the need for validation.

Just as the wind's destructive force can leave devastation in its path, the actions of the Malehufas of this world have consequences. The pain caused by shattered relationships lingers, and those affected must embark on a journey of healing and rebuilding trust.

In the tapestry of relationships, the presence of Malehufa serves as a reminder of the importance of nurturing and safeguarding connections. It highlights the significance of open communication, empathy, and understanding to counteract the destructive forces that seek to tear people apart.

Ultimately, while Malehufa may find momentary satisfaction in breaking relationships, true fulfilment and happiness are found in fostering love, respect and harmony among individuals, creating a tapestry of strong and resilient bonds.

My clarion call for you, my friends, is to protect your relationships from bad influence.

Pessimists, or negative thinkers, are people who consistently focus on the negative aspects of life. They have a pessimistic outlook on situations, events, and people, constantly looking for and dwelling on the negatives, flaws, or unfavourable outcomes.

Individuals may adopt such a mindset for a variety of reasons. Some may have had previous disappointments or traumas that shaped their perspective. Others' negative thinking patterns may have developed as a result of their upbringing, environment, or personal beliefs.

People who are constantly looking for flaws in their experiences often struggle to find joy, contentment, or optimism. They may have a habit of anticipating and focusing on potential problems, setbacks, or failures, which can limit their ability to appreciate the positives or see opportunities for growth and improvement.

This constant focus on the negative can have an impact not only on their own well-being and mental health but also on their interactions with others. It can strain relationships because the negativity is draining or off-putting to those around them. If you find yourself in such a situation, leave immediately.

Chapter Twenty-Four

Strength In Stillness

Once upon a time, there was a little seed planted in the ground. It was surrounded by other seeds, all eager to grow into beautiful plants. Days went by, and the seeds were filled with excitement, expecting to sprout and reach for the sun.

But the little seed remained still, seemingly dormant and motionless. The other seeds laughed and whispered, wondering why it didn't grow like the rest. They believed it was weak and incapable of becoming anything noteworthy.

As time passed, the seasons changed. The rain fell, and the sun shone brightly. The other seeds sprouted and grew into small plants, their leaves reaching towards the sky. The little seed, however, remained still, seemingly unchanged.

But beneath the surface, something remarkable was happening. The little seed was sending out roots, spreading deep into the ground, anchoring itself firmly. It was quietly gathering strength, drawing nutrients and water from the earth.

The Weight We Carry: A Blueprint for Dealing with Life's Burdens

One day, when the other plants were basking in their newfound height, a gentle breeze blew through the garden. The plants swayed and bent, their fragile stems struggling to withstand the wind's force. The little seed, however, stood firm and unmoved.

The other plants marvelled at the little seed's resilience. They realised that while they had grown tall quickly, their growth was superficial and lacked a strong foundation. The little seed, on the other hand, had focused on building strength from within.

As time went on, the little seed continued to grow, slowly but steadily. Its roots grew deeper and stronger, enabling it to withstand storms and adversity. Eventually, it burst through the surface, revealing a small yet beautifully formed plant.

The other plants admired the little seed's transformation. They realised that true strength was not always evident on the outside but stemmed from the quiet perseverance and solid foundation within.

And so, the little seed became a symbol of strength in stillness. It taught the other plants and all who witnessed its journey that sometimes, the most remarkable growth occurs when we find the strength to remain still, focus on inner development, and patiently gather the resources we need to thrive.

Be still. When you are calm, you can think more clearly and make rational decisions. You are less likely to be influenced by impulsive or emotional reactions, enabling you to assess situations objectively and choose the most appropriate course of action. This clear thinking helps in problem-solving, strategising and making sound judgements.

Be still, because calm people tend to have a higher level of emotional intelligence. They are self-aware, able to recognise and regulate their own emotions effectively. Additionally, they show empathy towards others, understanding their perspectives and responding with empathy and patience. This emotional intelligence helps in managing relationships, resolving conflicts, and building rapport with others.

It's important to note that being calm doesn't mean being passive or indifferent. It's about maintaining a sense of inner peace and composure while actively engaging with the world around you. By cultivating calmness, individuals can harness their strengths, make better decisions, and create an environment conducive to success.

Besides, you are not going to drive the car your friend drives at the same time. You will not build houses at the same time. You will not have family at the same time. You will not be promoted at the same time. Be still and pursue your plans, your time will come.

Chapter Twenty-Five

Pearls Before Swine

The phrase "pearls before swine" is a proverbial expression that comes from a biblical reference in the Gospel of Matthew (7:6). It is often used metaphorically to describe situations where valuable or precious things are offered or presented to individuals who are unable to appreciate or understand their worth.

The phrase suggests that some people may not recognise or value the significance of something valuable or meaningful when it is presented to them. Just as pigs, being animals known for their lack of discernment or appreciation, would disregard or trample on pearls, there are individuals who may disregard or fail to appreciate something valuable or important that is offered to them.

This expression is commonly used to caution against wasting one's efforts, time, or resources on individuals who are not receptive, open-minded, or capable of appreciating them. It implies that it is futile or unproductive to present something valuable to those who cannot understand or value its worth.

In a broader sense, "pearls before swine" can also serve as a metaphor for situations where efforts to share knowledge, wisdom, or beauty are met with indifference, ridicule, or rejection. It suggests that it is important to consider the audience's or recipient's ability and willingness to appreciate and understand what is being offered before investing significant time or effort into it.

Overall, the phrase "pearls before swine" serves as a reminder to be mindful of where we direct our energy, resources, and efforts and to recognise when it may be more beneficial to direct them towards those who can truly appreciate and benefit from them.

In short, I'm asking indirectly: *do you happy, naa?* (sic) Are you in a relationship or friendship where you are the only one making an effort? You cannot change someone; they must want to change. You are not a bad person or do not do enough; you are simply misfiring. Change your goal and focus your efforts on the right people.

Imagine you are a chef who has spent hours crafting a delicate, gourmet dish with exquisite flavours and presentation. However, you are invited to a gathering where the attendees have very limited culinary knowledge and appreciation. They prefer simple, fast-food-style dishes and have no interest in exploring the artistry and complexity of fine cuisine.

In this scenario, offering your meticulously prepared gourmet dish to the attendees would be like casting pearls before swine. Despite your efforts and the value you see in your creation, it would likely go unappreciated and even dismissed by the audience. They lack the palate and understanding to recognise the time, skill, and quality behind the dish, much like swine would disregard the beauty and worth of pearls.

The Weight We Carry: A Blueprint for Dealing with Life's Burdens

Chapter Twenty-Six

Not Immediately But Definitely

Imagine planting a seed in the ground. After carefully nurturing it with water, sunlight, and nutrients, you may not see any visible changes or growth for several weeks. However, if you continue to provide the necessary conditions for the seed to flourish, eventually it will sprout, develop roots, and grow into a strong, mature plant or tree.

In this analogy, the phrase "Not immediately but definitely" captures the idea that the growth and transformation of the seed may not be immediately evident, but with time and consistent care, it will undoubtedly flourish. Similarly, in various aspects of life, whether it's personal development, professional endeavours, or relationships, progress may not be immediately apparent, but with persistence and dedication, positive outcomes will eventually materialise.

You need to be patient, have perseverance, and trust in the process. It reminds us that some things take time to evolve and reach their full potential, and that the fruits of our efforts may not be immediate, but they are certainly achievable with continued commitment.

Do not get tired or stop believing.

Chapter Twenty-Seven

To Survive Or To Thrive?

I was inspired to write this piece after an apprentice frustrated me by making the perilous statement that he only wants the bare necessities in life. I believe he misunderstood some Bible concepts since he mentioned some lines from the Bible. I tried to persuade him to set higher goals, but he was adamant that he only wanted the bare minimum. I'm not sure what put him in survival mode, but I know it will be detrimental when he reaches the age of 30.

The title of this chapter, "To survive or to thrive," suggests a contrasting statement that presents two different levels of existence or accomplishment. It reflects the choice between merely staying alive or actively seeking growth, fulfilment, and success in various aspects of life.

Survival, in this context, refers to the basic instinct and effort to meet one's fundamental needs for food, shelter, safety, and security. It is about enduring and getting through challenging circumstances or situations. Survival mode often involves focusing on immediate concerns and ensuring basic necessities are met without necessarily striving for higher aspirations.

On the other hand, thriving goes beyond mere survival. It entails flourishing, progressing, and achieving a state of well-being, satisfaction, and personal growth. Thriving involves actively pursuing goals, embracing challenges, expanding one's potential, and finding fulfilment in different areas of life, such as relationships, career, health, and personal development.

While survival is essential and serves as a foundation, thriving represents a higher level of engagement and fulfilment. Thriving is about living a life of purpose, passion, and vitality, where individuals actively seek opportunities for growth, self-improvement, and realising their full potential.

It's important to note that the choice between survival and thriving is not always absolute, and circumstances can influence our focus at different times. There may be periods in life where survival becomes the primary concern, such as during emergencies or difficult situations. However, even during such times, the mindset of thriving can provide resilience and hope, guiding individuals towards finding opportunities for growth and seeking positive outcomes.

Chapter Twenty-Eight

Still, Black Tax

I would not have written this title had it not been for a couple of suicides by people who said their families demanded so much from them that they could not afford their own life plans. One that was close to home was the alleged suicide of a young man from Tshware village, who, to most of us, looked highly successful and happy. He was bubbly, and it seemed like all was going well in his teaching career.

I'm not sure how to put it, but I know it's a burden. Do we really want to be wealthy while having poor families or siblings? Would we be happy living in double-story city houses while our parents lived in shacks in villages without running water? Can we happily drive expensive cars while our parents and siblings go hungry before school or work?

What exactly is a black tax? Is it a sense of purpose or a burden?

Can we really abandon our siblings' educations and pursue our own until we can't? Is the black tax a punishment or a sign of progress?

Imagine if your parents considered you a burden and did not take you through school. What am I saying, though? I'm not sure how to explain it, but it is a depression trigger for many young adults.

Perhaps because I am a storyteller, allow me to tell you something, and I will not be held responsible for your interpretation. It doesn't matter what you think. Just a thought. I'll never know how difficult it is for you.

Imagine a relay race where each runner represents a generation in a family. The race track symbolises the journey towards success and prosperity. Now, in this particular race, some runners are given a head start—you—while others have to overcome hurdles and obstacles right from the beginning—your siblings and parents. This head start and these hurdles represent the systemic advantages or disadvantages that different families face.

As the race progresses, the runners who started with a head start maintain their lead, while those who faced hurdles must exert extra effort to catch up. However, there's an additional burden placed on some of the runners—the Black Tax. It's like an extra weight that they have to carry while running.

This weight represents the financial and emotional responsibilities that individuals from marginalised families often face due to historical and systemic disadvantages. It could include supporting family members financially, providing for extended family members, or taking on extra responsibilities due to limited resources.

As the race continues, the runners carrying the Black Tax struggle to keep up with their counterparts who are not burdened by the same responsibilities. They must find ways to balance their own aspirations and ambitions with the obligations they carry.

However, despite the challenges and the extra weight, these runners persevere. They work hard, showing resilience, determination, and resourcefulness. They learn to leverage their strengths, seek support from their community, and make sacrifices along the way.

Some runners manage to catch up, surpassing the initial head start of their counterparts. They break through the barriers and defy the odds, demonstrating the incredible potential and talent that exist within their families.

The race doesn't end there. As these individuals succeed, they become beacons of hope and inspiration for the next generation. They reach out their hands to lift others, offering support, mentorship, and resources. They understand the importance of breaking the cycle and creating opportunities for future runners, reducing the weight of the Black Tax for generations to come.

Aretse!

Chapter Twenty-Nine

Still, Pride Goes Before Destruction

The phrase "pride goes before destruction" is an idiom that originates from the biblical book of Proverbs in the Old Testament. The specific verse is Proverbs 16:18, which states, "Pride goes before destruction, a haughty spirit before a fall." This proverbial statement implies that when individuals become overly confident, arrogant, or excessively proud, it often leads to their downfall or negative consequences.

I think this is straight to the point. Let me not waste your time and move on to the next chapter. I just wanted to say that unchecked pride can cloud judgement, hinder personal growth, and lead to ruin. It serves as a reminder to remain humble, open-minded, and willing to learn from others, as these qualities contribute to long-term success and well-being.

Be kind.

Chapter Thirty

Loose Lips Sink Ships

In a small coastal town, Mazama worked as a radio operator for the Allied forces. Her role was crucial in transmitting coded messages and coordinating military operations. Mazama was diligent and respected among her colleagues for her unwavering commitment to the cause.

One day, Mazama attended a social gathering at a local pub. Amidst the merriment and excitement, she got carried away in a conversation with a stranger. Eager to impress, Mazama mentioned the upcoming secret mission that her unit was planning.

Unbeknownst to her, the stranger was a spy working for the enemy. His mission was to gather intelligence and disrupt Allied operations. Sensing an opportunity, he engaged Mazama further, coaxing her to reveal more details about the mission.

Caught up in the moment, Mazama let her guard down and shared classified information. She had inadvertently become a victim of loose lips. Little did she know that her momentary lapse in judgement would have grave consequences.

The spy quickly relayed the information to his superiors, who wasted no time in preparing a countermove. As a result, the secret mission Mazama had revealed was compromised. The enemy forces set up an ambush, leading to a significant loss of lives and equipment.

When Mazama discovered the devastating outcome of her indiscretion, she was overwhelmed with guilt and remorse. She realised the weight of her actions and the responsibility she held as a trusted member of the Allied forces.

Mazama's mistake served as a harsh reminder to her and her colleagues about the importance of maintaining strict confidentiality. It emphasised the need for discretion and caution when discussing sensitive information, even in seemingly innocuous settings. The incident reinforced the slogan "loose lips sink ships" as a powerful warning against the potential consequences of careless talk during wartime.

The phrase "loose lips sink ships" is a famous wartime slogan originating during World War II. It was used as a reminder for people to be cautious about sharing sensitive information that could potentially aid the enemy. It implies that careless or indiscreet talk can have severe consequences, including jeopardising the safety and success of military operations.

I know I took long to drive my point. I simply mean that certain things are better left unsaid.

Chapter Thirty-One

To Rob Peter To Pay Paul

The phrase "robbing Peter to pay Paul" is an idiomatic expression used to describe a situation where one solves a problem or fulfils a commitment by creating another problem or neglecting another commitment in the process. It implies that a person or entity is taking resources or benefits from one source to fulfil obligations or meet needs elsewhere, often resulting in a cycle of never-ending problems.

It originates from the historical practice of "robbing Peter's Church to pay Paul's Church." In mediaeval times, church buildings and monasteries were often funded by the contributions and donations of their parishioners. However, in some instances, funds allocated for one religious institution were redirected or used to support another, which could lead to neglect or a lack of resources for the original purpose.

It is applicable in various contexts, not limited to religious or financial matters. It can be used to describe situations where a solution or advantage is gained in one area at the expense of another.

For example, if a person is struggling to pay off one debt, they may resort to taking on additional debt or borrowing money from elsewhere to cover the original debt, ultimately creating a bigger financial burden.

In our lives, we lose so much by trying to take from where we are not supposed to in order to patch something else. In my undergraduate studies, in my second year, I stayed with one fellow from GaMothapo at MBD at the University of Limpopo in a shared room. Okay, my residence is not important in this story. I am trying to set the scene, but I think I am losing track of my thoughts. Next door, there was a young couple. The brother bought out his roommate to stay with her struggling girlfriend. He paid the roommate a monthly fee to stay away. Where he stayed, I do not know, lest I incriminate myself. Mosima and Michael, who have been together for several years, behaved like a couple of moons. They have always been supportive of each other's dreams and ambitions. Mosima has been working hard to build her career as a graphic designer, while Michael pursues his passion for music and dreams of starting his own band.

As Mosima's career begins to take off, she finds herself in high demand, receiving lucrative job offers and opportunities for advancement. Meanwhile, Michael's musical pursuits are not as successful. He struggles to find consistent gigs and often relies on odd jobs at the computer lab and events as an usher to make ends meet.

In an effort to support Michael's dreams and alleviate his financial burdens, Mosima takes on extra freelance projects and works longer hours. She believes that by sacrificing her own time and energy, she can help support Michael's aspirations and give him the opportunity to focus on his music.

The Weight We Carry: A Blueprint for Dealing with Life's Burdens

However, as Mosima becomes consumed by her work commitments, she starts to neglect her own well-being and her relationship with Michael. She has less time and energy for quality time together, emotional support, and maintaining a healthy work-life balance. The constant juggling of responsibilities and the strain of taking on more work for financial stability began to take a toll on her mental and physical health.

Meanwhile, Michael, while appreciative of Mosima's efforts, begins to feel guilty for not contributing equally to the relationship. He becomes frustrated with his own lack of progress and feels pressure to succeed to justify Mosima's sacrifices. Over time, the relationship becomes imbalanced, with Mosima constantly robbing Peter (her own well-being, personal time, and emotional needs) to pay Paul (Michael's dreams and financial stability). The lack of reciprocity and emotional neglect led to resentment, communication breakdowns, and a growing distance between Mosima and Michael.

I remember this very well: Mosima's well-intentioned actions to support Michael's dreams and financial stability end up straining their relationship. By consistently prioritising Michael's needs over her own, she robs herself of the emotional nourishment and self-care necessary for a healthy partnership. Ultimately, the cycle of neglect and imbalance takes a toll on both individuals and the relationship as a whole.

In essence, "robbing Peter to pay Paul" signifies a temporary or short-term fix that fails to address the underlying issues and can perpetuate a cycle of problems. It emphasises the need for holistic and sustainable solutions that consider the bigger picture rather than simply shifting resources or problems around. Anyway, they never found the balance, lost their feelings for each other, and broke up. You get the point, right?

Chapter Thirty-Two

Be My Guest

People will occasionally coerce you into doing things that you don't want to do. You ultimately decide to concur because you want to fit in. They occasionally threaten you. I've learnt to maintain my integrity ever since I first decided to say, "Be my guest."

Learn to use the phrase; there is so much freedom after saying these words.

Chapter Thirty-Three

Sankofa

Sankofa is a word derived from the Akan language, spoken by the Akan people of Ghana. It is a concept that represents the idea of "going back to fetch" or "returning to the past in order to move forward." The symbol associated with Sankofa is often depicted as a bird with its head turned backward while its feet face forward.

Sankofa is often used to express the importance of learning from the past, valuing and preserving one's history, and using that knowledge to shape the future. It emphasises the idea that in order to move forward, one must understand and acknowledge their roots, history, and cultural heritage.

The concept of Sankofa has gained significance beyond the Akan culture and has been adopted as a symbol and philosophy by people of African descent around the world.

The Weight We Carry: A Blueprint for Dealing with Life's Burdens

It serves as a reminder to honour and draw strength from one's cultural heritage while actively shaping a better future. In addition to its cultural significance, Sankofa has been used as a symbol in various contexts, such as art, literature, and social activism, to promote ideas of self-awareness, self-empowerment, and cultural pride. Let's bring it home a bit. You're embarking on a journey through a dense forest. As you walk along the path, you come across a signpost pointing in two directions: "Future" and "Past." Intrigued, you decide to follow the arrow pointing towards the past.

As you venture into the past, you discover remnants of ancient civilisations, artefacts, and the stories of those who came before. You learn about their triumphs, struggles, and wisdom. This journey allows you to gain a deeper understanding of your roots, cultural heritage, and the experiences that have shaped you. Armed with this newfound knowledge, you turn back towards the present, but this time, you walk with a renewed sense of purpose. The lessons learned from the past empower you to make informed decisions, avoid repeating mistakes, and build a better future.

The forest represents the timeline of your life, while the signpost symbolises the concept of Sankofa, inviting you to explore the past to inform your present and future. Just as Sankofa encourages you to learn from the past, by understanding where you come from, you can navigate your path forward more effectively.

What is it that you feel like going back to in your life? When pursuing success, it's easy to become consumed by our goals and aspirations, often neglecting important aspects of life due to naivety or oversight.

Here are a few important things that people sometimes overlook in their quest for success:

1. **Relationships:** Building and maintaining meaningful relationships with family, friends, and loved ones is crucial for overall happiness and well-being. Neglecting these connections can lead to feelings of loneliness and regret, even if you achieve success in other areas of life.

2. **Health and Well-being:** Neglecting your physical and mental health can have long-term consequences. Prioritise self-care, exercise, proper nutrition, and sufficient rest. Ignoring these aspects can lead to burnout, health issues, and a diminished quality of life.

3. **Work-Life Balance:** Striving for success often means dedicating significant time and effort to your work or career. However, it's important to maintain a healthy work-life balance. Neglecting personal time, hobbies, and leisure activities can lead to stress, decreased productivity, and a lack of fulfillment outside of work.

4. **Personal Values and Integrity:** Success should not come at the cost of compromising your values and integrity. It's essential to stay true to yourself, make ethical choices, and act with integrity throughout your journey. Neglecting these principles can lead to inner conflicts, damaged relationships, and a shallow sense of achievement.

5. **Enjoying the Present Moment:** While it's important to set goals and work towards them, it's equally crucial to enjoy the journey and appreciate the present moment. Success can be a long-term pursuit, and if you constantly focus on the future, you may miss out on the joys and experiences of the present.

Chapter Thirty-Four

A Paycheck Away From Poverty

As I started working, I realised that if I were to be fired, I would be like someone who never worked. It is highly possible to be a hobo. I felt like I was walking on a tightrope without a safety net. Just as a tightrope walker balances precariously, one wrong step or unexpected gust of wind can send them plummeting to the ground, risking their safety and well-being. Similarly, living hand to mouth means constantly teetering on the edge of financial instability, with little room for error or unforeseen circumstances.

The tightrope represents the fragile balance between income and expenses. Each step taken must be carefully calculated to ensure survival and meet basic needs. Any unexpected expense or reduction in income can disrupt this delicate equilibrium, leading to a downward spiral of debt, stress and limited opportunities. Moreover, just as a tightrope walker cannot afford to look too far ahead or plan for the long term while maintaining their immediate balance, individuals living hand to mouth struggle to think beyond their immediate needs.

They are trapped in day-to-day survival mode, unable to invest in their future or build a solid foundation for financial security. Without a safety net, the risks are amplified. Any unexpected setback—a medical emergency, job loss, or major expense—can have devastating consequences, pushing individuals further into poverty and making it even more challenging to escape the hand-to-mouth cycle.

Ultimately, the tightrope walker's goal is to reach the other side, where stability, security, and peace of mind await. Similarly, individuals living hand to mouth strive for a better life, free from constant stress and uncertainty. However, just as a tightrope walker requires external support systems and safety measures to mitigate risks, individuals in such circumstances need access to financial education, social safety nets, and opportunities for upward mobility to break free from the dangers of living hand to mouth.

If you were to be fired from your job today, would you survive for the next three months? See what I mean? Make a plan; passive income in this economy is a ticking time bomb. One mistake—hmmm!

Chapter Thirty-Five

The Fire-Fighting Approach

If there is one thing I have realised, it is that fighting fire is not a very helpful process. I've seen houses burn to the ground even when the fire department was nearby and fighting it. During my childhood, my village used to burn down people accused of witchcraft; the blazes could never be extinguished. When fields burn, they always burn completely, despite attempts to put out the fire.

This prompted me to consider the concept of firefighting and its effectiveness. It doesn't work very well. It is never a well-done job; it is always an attempt.

As a homeowner with a fire alarm system installed in your house, the fire alarm is designed to detect smoke and alert you in case of a fire. In this scenario, the firefighting approach would be akin to relying solely on the fire alarm to address fire emergencies.

With the firefighting approach, you don't take any proactive measures to prevent fires. You don't regularly inspect electrical wiring, maintain fire extinguishers, or educate yourself on fire safety.

Instead, you wait for the fire alarm to go off, indicating that a fire has already started, before you take action. When the alarm sounds, you quickly grab a fire extinguisher and attempt to put out the fire, or you call the fire department to handle the situation.

While the fire alarm is essential for alerting you to immediate dangers, relying solely on it without taking preventive measures can have serious consequences. By neglecting fire prevention, you increase the likelihood of fires occurring and put yourself and your property at greater risk.

In contrast, a proactive approach to fire safety involves taking preventive measures to reduce the chances of a fire breaking out in the first place. You regularly check electrical systems, maintain fire extinguishers, install smoke detectors in every room, and develop an evacuation plan. Additionally, you educate yourself and your family members on fire safety practices, such as not leaving candles unattended or overloading electrical outlets.

By adopting a proactive approach, you significantly decrease the likelihood of fires occurring and minimise potential damage. You're not solely relying on the fire alarm to alert you to a crisis; instead, you've taken steps to prevent fires and protect yourself and your property.

In the same way, the firefighting approach in other areas of life or business involves reacting to crises and addressing immediate problems as they occur. However, it's essential to combine this reactive mindset with proactive measures to prevent issues, minimise risks, and create a more stable and secure environment. Imagine you're a student preparing for an important exam that will determine your overall grade for the course. The fire-fighting approach in this scenario would involve waiting until the last minute to start studying and only focusing on cramming information right before the exam.

With the fire-fighting approach, you haven't been proactive in managing your time and studying effectively throughout the semester. Instead, you've ignored assignments, skipped classes, and neglected to review course materials. As the exam date approaches, you realise the gravity of the situation and start panicking. You frantically try to learn as much as possible in a short amount of time, sacrificing sleep and neglecting other responsibilities.

While this firefighting approach may provide some short-term results, it comes with several drawbacks. You're more likely to feel overwhelmed, stressed, and exhausted. Additionally, the information you cram may not be retained effectively, and you may not fully grasp the concepts necessary for long-term understanding and application.

Firefighters in my village understand that once a fire starts, it will never be extinguished. They clean up around important plantations so that the fire does not break through and spread throughout the field and can be contained within the area where it started. As firefighters, they do not rely on water and extinguishers, but rather plan ahead of time because they know that a fire can start at any time.

In our lives, dealing with crises on a regular basis indicates that we regard every day as a gift and never prepare for it. We prefer to solve problems rather than create solutions. A life lived in this manner frequently buckles under pressure and never reaches a satisfying stage.

Chapter Thirty-Six

When An Adult Doesn't Want To Mature

Peter Pan Syndrome, also known as Peter Pan Complex or Syndrome, is a pop psychology concept that refers to an individual's inability or unwillingness to grow up and take on adult responsibilities. It is named after the character Peter Pan, created by J.M. Barrie in his play and novel "Peter Pan."

People with Peter Pan Syndrome typically exhibit childlike behaviours, resist societal expectations, and avoid the responsibilities associated with adulthood. They may display a fear of commitment, a desire for independence and freedom, and a reluctance to settle down into stable careers or relationships. They often seek immediate gratification, engage in impulsive or reckless behaviour, and have difficulty facing the realities of life. While Peter Pan Syndrome is not an officially recognised psychological disorder, there are certain signs or behaviours that are commonly associated with it. It's important to note that these signs or symptoms can vary among individuals, and the presence of these behaviours does not necessarily indicate the presence of Peter Pan Syndrome.

Here are some characteristics often associated with Peter Pan Syndrome:

1. **Fear of commitment:** Individuals with Peter Pan Syndrome may struggle with committing to long-term relationships, careers, or other significant life choices. They may avoid making commitments and prefer to maintain their freedom and independence.

2. **Reluctance to take on adult responsibilities:** People with Peter Pan Syndrome often resist or avoid the responsibilities associated with adulthood, such as paying bills, managing finances, or taking care of their own well-being. They may rely on others to meet their needs or expect others to take care of them.

3. **Desire for immediate gratification:** Individuals with Peter Pan Syndrome may prioritise immediate pleasure and gratification over long-term goals or delayed gratification. They may engage in impulsive or reckless behaviour without considering the consequences.

4. **Difficulty with long-term planning:** Planning for the future and setting long-term goals may be challenging for individuals with Peter Pan Syndrome. They may prefer to live in the present moment and avoid thinking about the future or making concrete plans.

5. **Preference for fantasy and escapism:** Like the character of Peter Pan, individuals with this syndrome may have a strong inclination towards fantasy and escapism. They may use imagination, daydreaming, or engaging in childlike activities as a way to avoid the realities and challenges of adult life.

Chapter Thirty-Seven

The Looking Self Glass

The Looking-Glass Self is a sociological concept developed by Charles Cooley. It refers to the idea that a person's self-concept and social identity are shaped by how they believe others perceive them. Cooley proposed this theory based on his observations of children's social development and the role of social interaction in the formation of self-identity.

According to the Looking-Glass Self theory, individuals imagine how they appear to others and then interpret the reactions of those people to create their own self-perception. The process involves three main steps.

Imagining how one appears to others

Individuals imagine how they are perceived by others, considering aspects such as physical appearance, behaviour, and social interactions.

Interpreting the reactions of others

Individuals interpret the reactions and feedback they receive from others in response to their perceived appearance. These reactions can include verbal and nonverbal cues, praise, criticism, or indifference.

Developing a self-concept

Based on their interpretation of others' reactions, individuals develop a self-concept, which includes their beliefs, values, and evaluations of themselves. This self-concept is influenced by the perceived judgments and expectations of others.

In this process, individuals rely on social interactions and feedback to shape their self-perception and construct their social identity. The Looking-Glass Self theory highlights the importance of social context and the influence of others in the formation of individual identity.

Effectively, the ideas and feelings that people have about themselves — their self-concept or self-image — are developed in response to their perception and internalisation of how others perceive and evaluate them.

Let's go back to the images I shared in the introduction. You are standing in front of a mirror, and you feel like there are other people in the room observing you. You are trying to understand how you appear to them and how they perceive you. As you interact with them, you pay attention to their reactions, expressions and comments.

- The mirror represents your perception of yourself.
- The other people you think about in the room represent the social environment and the people you interact with.
- Your reflection in the mirror is how you imagine you appear to others.
- The reactions, expressions and comments you have in your mind, of the people in the room, represent the feedback and cues you receive, or expect to, from others.

Based on their reactions, you interpret their judgements, whether positive or negative. If you think they will be impressed by your appearance or actions, you may develop a positive self-image. On the other hand, if they criticise or ignore you, you might perceive yourself in a more negative light.

Over time, these interactions and feedback shape your self-concept. Your self-perception is not solely based on your own thoughts and beliefs but is influenced by the reflections you receive from the people around you. Thus, just as the mirror reflects your image, the perception of others becomes a "looking-glass" through which you construct your self-identity.

The mirror and the reactions of others serve as the elements that contribute to the formation of your self-perception, highlighting the interconnectedness between social interaction and the development of self-identity.

I've noticed a sad trend in social media and WhatsApp statuses. Young and old alike post pictures and use the number of likes to identify with them. Social media is typically interested in hilarious, extreme posts, and people think less of themselves when they post decent and inspirational posts.

They end up posting nudes, wearing near-naked fashion trends, and purchasing expensive and designer clothes in order to receive likes and feel good about themselves. We keep wondering why depression is so prevalent. It's partly because we see ourselves through the likes and followers we receive on social media.

We invest so much time in creating content that does not define who we are, just to get more likes. We lose our moral compass and make light of sensitive issues because it makes sense online. We troll each other because it keeps people on our pages for gossip and fun. We spend more time at groove trying to appear to have a "soft life" while struggling to get by, and we end up doing everything we can to be in those spaces.

Social media have become our looking self glass, and constructing self-value solely or primarily based on social media can have several potential dangers and negative consequences.

Validation and self-esteem

Relying on social media for validation and self-esteem can be risky. Social media platforms often promote a culture of seeking external validation through likes, comments and followers. When self-worth becomes dependent on these metrics, individuals may experience fluctuations in self-esteem based on the feedback received. This can lead to feelings of inadequacy, anxiety and a constant need for validation.

I was disheartened at how the Americans on Instagram trolled Uncle Waffles about her weave, make-up, dental formula, etc. She was made by the very same social media, wearing the same things and exactly how she is. Now, the same platform tries to ridicule her self-identity.

A parody account on Twitter called Chris Excel brought Lerato "LKG" Kganyago to tears on several occasions because she believed the troller's perception or feedback about her being "Bonang Lite" defined her career and talents, and she wanted to defend herself.

Comparison and envy

Social media is a breeding ground for comparison. People often showcase the best aspects of their lives, which can create an illusion of perfection and success. Constant exposure to others' highlight reels may lead individuals to compare themselves unfavourably, fostering feelings of envy and dissatisfaction and a distorted perception of reality. This can negatively impact self-image and contribute to a constant need to measure up to unrealistic standards.

Relationships fail and marriages end because people see occasional nice outings as reality and want to imitate them. They put their partners under pressure to live like the people they see on reels, and they end up cheating to get what they want. They end up dating multiple partners so that they can be provided with various reels, such as road trips that require someone with a car, VIP access that requires a DJ, a penthouse that requires a tenderpreneur, nice food that requires another person, and so on, because one person can never afford all of these things on a consistent basis.

FOMO and anxiety

The curated nature of social media can intensify the fear of missing out (FOMO). Seeing others' seemingly exciting experiences and achievements can induce anxiety and a sense of being left out. It may create a constant pressure to participate in or showcase experiences to gain social approval, which can detract from genuine personal fulfillment and happiness.

Inauthentic self-presentation

Social media encourages selective self-presentation, where individuals highlight positive aspects of their lives while downplaying or hiding vulnerabilities and struggles. This curated self-image can lead to a sense of disconnection between the online persona and the true self, contributing to feelings of loneliness, isolation, and a lack of authenticity.

Mental health impact

Research suggests a link between excessive social media use and mental health issues such as depression, anxiety and low self-esteem. Constant comparison, negative social interactions, cyberbullying, and the pressure to maintain a perfect online image can all contribute to these negative effects on mental well-being.

To mitigate these dangers, it is important to cultivate a healthy relationship with social media:

Practice self-awareness: Be mindful of how social media affects your emotions, self-perception, and overall well-being. Recognise the difference between online personas and real-life experiences.

Limit screen time: Set boundaries for social media use to avoid excessive exposure and potential negative effects. Allocate time for offline activities, self-care, and real-world connections.

Seek genuine connections: Foster meaningful relationships and connections beyond social media. Cultivate real-life interactions and prioritise quality interactions over quantity.

Focus on self-care: Engage in activities that promote self-esteem, self-compassion, and personal growth. Develop a strong sense of self based on your values, interests and goals rather than seeking validation solely through social media.

Practice digital detox: Take regular breaks from social media to recharge, reflect and reconnect with the present moment. This can help reduce dependency and restore a healthier perspective on self-value.

Chapter Thirty-Eight

Jump Before You're Pushed

In a small village called Makgopheng in GaMamabolo, there lived a young shepherd named Mohlokomedi. He tended to a flock of sheep with great care, ensuring their safety and well-being day after day.

Mohlokomedi had heard tales of a powerful storm that was predicted to hit the village in the coming weeks. The storm was said to bring torrential rains and fierce winds that could devastate the village and pose a grave danger to his sheep. Determined to protect his flock, Mohlokomedi decided to take action before the storm arrived. He believed in the old adage, "Jump Before You're Pushed."

With urgency in his heart, Mohlokomedi sought the guidance of an elderly, wise woman known for her deep connection to nature. She shared her wisdom and advised him to lead his sheep to a hidden valley on the other side of the mountain. The valley was sheltered by towering cliffs, which provided natural protection from the harsh elements.

Mohlokomedi wasted no time. He gathered his sheep and began the arduous journey through rugged terrain, navigating the treacherous paths of the mountain. It was a challenging endeavour, but his determination to ensure the safety of his flock fuelled his strength.

As Mohlokomedi and his sheep finally reached the hidden valley, the storm clouds loomed ominously overhead. The winds grew stronger, and raindrops started to fall. With each passing moment, the storm intensified, unleashing its fury on the village.

But in the sheltered valley, Mohlokomedi's flock found refuge. The cliffs shielded them from the harsh winds, and the valley's natural contours provided ample protection from the raging storm. As the storm raged outside, Mohlokomedi stood there, watching over his flock with a sense of relief and gratitude.

The "Jump Before You're Pushed" concept is used to describe a situation where someone takes preemptive action or makes a decision before they are forced or pressured into doing so by external circumstances. It implies that by acting proactively, one can maintain some control over their situation and avoid being caught off guard or put in a disadvantageous position.

The phrase draws upon the idea of someone standing on the edge of a metaphorical cliff, knowing that they might be pushed off at any moment. Instead of waiting for that push, they choose to jump on their own terms, taking control of their destiny and potentially avoiding a worse outcome.

In a broader sense, the analogy can be applied to various situations where individuals or organisations anticipate an undesirable or inevitable event and take proactive measures to mitigate its effects or create a more favourable outcome.

It emphasises the importance of being proactive, anticipating challenges, and taking action before external forces dictate the terms of the situation. When you notice that they are about to fire you, begin looking for new employment. If you can tell that your partner does not appreciate you, leave before they tell you that you are no longer their love. You can detect jealousy in a friend; keep your distance before they poison you.

Pitso Mosimane always leaves when he begins to feel undervalued. He leaves with no blemishes on his record. Ruud Krol left Orlando Pirates after winning a double treble. He knew he'd lose everything if he was fired the following season because Prates didn't buy enough players while selling key players. If your partner starts beating you up, get out before you're beaten to a pulp.

It's simple: you can always tell when things aren't going well. Do not linger in situations that require you to move.

Chapter Thirty-Nine

Feather Dusters Were Once Peacocks

A fashion trend that becomes extremely popular and receives widespread acclaim in the present. People adore it; fashion magazines feature it prominently, and it becomes a symbol of style and sophistication. However, as time goes by and fashion evolves, tastes change and new trends emerge. What was once considered fashionable may eventually be seen as outdated or even ridiculed. This is not about fashion.

Let me get to the title and bring it home. In a land known for its breath-taking peacocks, there was a wise and resourceful community. They marvelled at the magnificent plumage of these proud birds, with their shimmering, iridescent feathers that seemed to capture the sunlight and reflect it in a mesmerising dance of colours.

One day, the people of this community faced a peculiar problem. Their homes and belongings were constantly besieged by dust and dirt, and they yearned for a solution to keep their surroundings clean and pristine. Inspired by the beauty of the peacock feathers, they embarked on a quest to find a way to harness their qualities for a practical purpose.

Driven by their ingenuity, the community set out to collect fallen peacock feathers from the forest floor. They carefully gathered the discarded feathers, knowing that each one carried the essence of the majestic birds that once wore them proudly. With utmost respect for the birds and their natural habitat, they ensured that no harm came to them.

Back in the village, the skilled artisans of the community worked diligently. They delicately cleaned and prepared the peacock feathers, removing any impurities and arranging them in a way that allowed their natural beauty to shine through. They attached these feathers to handles, creating what would become known as feather dusters.

The people marvelled at the transformation that had taken place. The once majestic peacock feathers, which once adorned the regal creatures, were now serving a humble yet essential purpose. These feather dusters became cherished tools in every household, allowing the community to maintain cleanliness and order in their homes.

The majestic creatures with grandeur are now used to remove dust. Your beauty, talent, honour, aura, and wealth could all be swept away, leaving you as a mere tool, the polar opposite of what you were born to be. Avoid them all and be humble.

Chapter Forty

Unlike Charges

The "Unlike Charges" concept is used to explain the attraction between positive and negative charges in physics. According to this, positive and negative charges are similar to the north and south poles of magnets, where opposite poles attract each other and like poles repel each other.

Let's say you have two magnets—one has a "+" sign, and the other has a "-" sign. When you bring these magnets close to each other, they will pull together and stick. This is because the opposite poles, the "+" and "-", attract each other.

For example, if you rub a balloon on your hair, the balloon becomes charged with static electricity. Your hair has the opposite charge, so when you hold the balloon near your hair, they are attracted to each other. The hair stands up towards the balloon because of this attraction between unlike charges.

In everyday life, the concept of unlike charges can help explain why people with different personalities or opinions can be drawn to each other. Just like magnets or electric charges, our differences can create a pull or curiosity that brings us together and allows us to learn from one another.

We avoid people who are different from us because we are afraid of learning new things. The most intelligent and progressive people understand that diversification in life is the ultimate determiner of our desired future. Friendships with people who do the same things you do limit your chances of success. You become conditioned to believe that anything other than what you know is unrealistic or impossible. You are afraid of even the simplest tasks and are unwilling to leave your comfort zone.

In today's world, a single skill is worthless. For a job posting, for example, you'd realise that the skillset required is interdisciplinary and complements one another. A person who develops multiple personalities has a better chance of negotiating their way out of difficult situations.

Begin to spread your wings and recognise that the entire world is the sum of its ecosystems, and you must understand the connections. Stop limiting yourself to people who do what you do; in fact, you should repel them because you can do what they can. You are aware of what they are aware of. As a result, most people in their workplaces are not innovative and are stuck in their ways of doing things, even when situations call for new ways of doing things. They don't know where to begin, who to approach, or with whom to collaborate. They are unaware that there is no energy in likeness.

Chapter Forty-One

The Dangers of The Beginning and End

The odds of dying as an aircraft passenger are almost too small to calculate. However, if you do die in a plane crash, it will likely happen during the first three minutes or the last eight minutes of the flight. The takeoff and ascent make up just 2% of the entire flight but account for 13% of all fatal accidents. Landings account for about 4% of the average flight but are responsible for half, if not more, of fatal accidents. *This is because takeoffs last 30 to 35 seconds.* If a problem arises, the pilot has almost no time to decide what to do. This significantly increases the chances of a dangerous error taking place, and the same can be said for the landing phase. Ultimately, it's both easier and safer for a plane to cruise than to land or take off.

Imagine you're in the air and both engines shut down because of the high velocity; the plane will continue to glide. A typical airliner loses about a mile (1.6 km) in altitude for every 10 (16 km) it moves forward, giving the pilot a little over eight minutes to react. When aviation accidents do occur, they are typically caused by a combination of factors, primarily human error, mechanical failure, and inclement weather.

Human error is the most common cause, accounting for about 50% of all accidents.

Mechanical failures alone do happen, but they account for only a small proportion of airline accidents.

And just as driving becomes more dangerous in bad weather, so does flying. Although today's airliners are able to safely operate in nearly any weather condition, small aircraft have to be far less careful.

Even in the journey of life, our terrible experiences are in the begging of the journey and the end. Most businesses closed down before their first anniversary. Most marriages collapsed at the honeymoon session. Most pregnancies miscarry in the first trimester or in the labour room.

I am beginning to sound like a pessimist. Forgive me. The point is that we have to start well and prepare to finish well if we are to succeed in life. There is no such thing, as I will see as time goes by. I promise not to talk in riddles after this last scenario. I just feel like it will make more sense to marry the aeroplane analogy with an actual experience you have had. Not that I am saying you have not been on a plane; well, it could be true.

Let us look at life itself. There are three trimesters in pregnancy, and each one has distinctive foetal developments. A pregnancy is considered full-term at 40 weeks; infants delivered before the end of week 37 are considered premature. Premature infants may have problems with their growth and development, as well as difficulties breathing and digesting.

First Trimester (0 to 13 Weeks)

The first trimester is crucial to the baby's development. During this period, the baby's body structure and organ systems develop. A woman then begins to no longer think about herself but mostly about her future self, which is being a mother. For many, there is the 'you' who you would like to be and then, more consistently, the 'you' that you are.

These two versions of yourself are not always aligned. If they were, we would all be superheroes. Disillusionment may follow about the number of things you "could" have done if only you had been persistent in your endeavours. Pregnancy forces the mother to change her lifestyle and some behaviours simply because most miscarriages and birth defects occur during this period.

The same happens to all of us. We are all going to be pregnant with some ideas about who we want to become and what we want the future to look like. Like the body of the mother undergoing major changes during the first trimester, the initial stages of goal-setting should make you want to look at yourself and think, "What do I need to do to safeguard my child?" You must then have so many ideas that confuse you, questions about how you would get there, how to start, where to go, who to tell, etc.

These are symptoms of conceiving a goal. What you hear, who you consult about your dream, and how you start will determine the success of your plans. Just like when a pregnant woman experiences changes in her body that often cause a variety of symptoms, including nausea, fatigue, breast tenderness, and frequent urination. Although these are common pregnancy symptoms, every woman has a different experience. For example, while some may experience an increased energy level during this period, others may feel very tired and emotional.

Even if someone else has achieved your dream by doing this and that, that does not mean it will always be so for you. Instead of copying what has worked, find out what works for you and in what environment. I know you're not reinventing the wheel, but at the same time, you're not using a worn-out tyre.

For these symptoms or concerns you will have as you begin to carry out your dream or vision, you need to know the following:

Clarity: Goals need to be specific.

When we have a dream about something or an invention, the first mistake we make is thinking that we can make it all on our own. We lack pure clarity about how far our vision can go and how to guide it in the process. A mentor is important in this regard.

Just like how a pregnant woman would have a pregnancy notebook (card) that defines her journey. The pregnancy 'notes' is the book in which all the information about medical history and pregnancy is recorded.

During the first antenatal appointment or talking to the mentor about your vision, called the booking appointment, your midwife will start a record. You do not explain how you got pregnant, but you start with the pregnancy. Do not wholly reveal to your mentor what your vision is, but be concerned about knowing how a vision is taken care of. This is called your 'notes'. At every appointment, your midwife or doctor will record what happens in your notes. As you navigate the goal-achieving process, note everything down.

You will usually take care of your notes. Take good care of them, as usually there is no copy. Keep them with you at all times in case of an emergency, and ask if there's anything you don't understand.

This is you learning the road to success and not deferring any process to the following day because you only have one shot at life.

Your notes will also usually have telephone numbers for you to use if you need to speak to anyone, a space to write the date and time of your next appointment, and a record of what you told the midwife in the booking appointment. Your network is your net worth. A business learning journey would need a lot of people with different expertise. Gather as many contacts as possible and know who you can talk to. We often lose sight of our dreams because we tell a lot of the wrong people.

Second Trimester (14 to 26 Weeks)

The second trimester of pregnancy is often called the "golden period" because many of the unpleasant effects of early pregnancy disappear. During the second trimester, you're likely to experience decreased nausea, better sleep patterns, and an increased energy level. However, you may experience a whole new set of symptoms, such as back pain, abdominal pain, leg cramps, constipation and heartburn.

Somewhere between 16 weeks and 20 weeks, you may feel your baby's first fluttering movements.

Many people at this stage, where they start to make a bit of money and can feel and see the success of the process, begin to show off. They begin to focus on the output and not necessarily on the whole process. Although it is not too dangerous to turn things around, you can miss important growth prospects. Never overgrow the process.

Third Trimester (27 to 40 Weeks)

You have now reached your final stretch of pregnancy and are probably very excited and anxious for the birth of your baby. Some of the physical symptoms you may experience during this period include shortness of breath, hemorrhoids, urinary incontinence, varicose veins and sleeping problems.

As you progress through life, remember the fundamental principles of doing what is right even when no one is looking. You should not drink and drive. Do not gossip about others. Do not belittle others. So many lives have been cut short as a result of signs of success. When people appear to have it all in life, they let down their guard.

Chapter Forty-Two

Cracks Success Will Never Fill

Let me tell you a story. *Le ka no re keleketla, ge le nyaka!* In the busy city of Polokwane, there lived a young and ambitious artist named Lebogang. Lebogang was exceptionally talented and dedicated to her craft. She spent years honing her skills and pursuing success in the art world. Her work gained recognition through exhibitions and prestigious awards. From the outside, it seemed like Lebogang had it all: fame, fortune and a thriving career.

However, deep within Lebogang's heart, there were cracks that success could never fill. She had always carried a sense of emptiness and a longing for deeper connections and purpose. Lebogang's success brought external validation, but it failed to mend the emotional voids she felt.

One day, while attending an art gala, Lebogang met an elderly woman named Lesedi. Lesedi, a wise and compassionate soul, saw through Lebogang's façade of success. She recognised the cracks within Lebogang's spirit and felt compelled to help her.

The Weight We Carry: A Blueprint for Dealing with Life's Burdens

Lesedi invited Lebogang to her humble cottage on the outskirts of the city. Surrounded by nature's serenity, they spent days engaging in heartfelt conversations and soul-searching. Lebogang began to realise that her pursuit of success had overshadowed other important aspects of her life—her relationships, self-growth, and inner happiness.

Through Lesedi's guidance, Lebogang embarked on a journey of self-discovery. She started exploring her emotions, confronting her past traumas, and rebuilding meaningful connections with loved ones. Lebogang realised that success alone could never mend her brokenness; it could only serve as a temporary distraction.

As Lebogang delved deeper into her personal growth, she discovered her true passions and a desire to create art that carried a message of love, healing, and authenticity. She no longer sought external validation but focused on creating art that resonated with her soul.

What am I telling you? That no matter how successful you can be, you can never outgrow your family. In my neighbourhood, there was a man who seemed to have everything in life, so it seemed. He lived in mansions, if not penthouses, in the city. His mother lived in the village and happened to die. The people in the community refused to dig her mother's grave because it was never part of the community's practises, like paying homage.

As much as he could afford an excavator to dig the grave, it was not a dignified way of sending someone off. In villages, we use what we call *diphiri* (grave diggers). Her money and success were meaningless, and he seemed to be the most uncomfortable person in the area. Success is not the solution to everything.

Let me give you one more instance. A beautiful vase represents your life. Success can be likened to colourful flowers that you place inside the vase, adding beauty and vibrancy to it. As you achieve your goals and experience external accomplishments, these flowers represent the external validation and rewards that success brings.

However, even with a vase full of beautiful flowers, there may still be cracks in the vase itself. These cracks symbolise the deeper aspects of life that success may not fully address. The cracks represent emotional voids, personal growth, purpose and meaning, health and well-being, and inner happiness.

No matter how many flowers you fill the vase with, they cannot repair the cracks. These cracks require separate attention and effort. They may need to be addressed through personal reflection, therapy, building meaningful relationships, prioritising self-care, or finding a sense of purpose beyond external achievements.

In order to have a truly fulfilling life, it's important to acknowledge and work on filling these cracks while pursuing success. By taking a holistic approach and tending to the vase itself, not just the flowers, you can create a life that is both externally successful and internally fulfilling.

Bjale gona ke dumela gore le nkwele!

Chapter Forty-Three

The Law of Energy

According to the law of conservation of energy, energy cannot be destroyed. It can only be transformed from one form to another or transferred from one object to another. This principle is a fundamental concept in physics.

The conservation of energy states that the total amount of energy in an isolated system remains constant over time. Energy may change its form or be transferred between different objects or systems, but the total energy within the closed system remains constant.

For example, when you burn wood, chemical potential energy is converted into heat energy and light energy. Some of this heat energy can be used to generate electricity, which can then be used to power various devices. The total amount of energy in this process remains the same, even though it has undergone a transformation from one form to another.

So, energy cannot be destroyed but can only be converted or transferred in accordance with the law of conservation of energy. Okay, here I go again, taking forever to make a point.

I am just saying, stop hoping that loving someone more will create the same energy in them or that staying in a toxic relationship and being a good person will destroy their bad traits. The energy you get from them is all they have; it can never be altered but can only take different forms. The minute you feel like their energy towards you is not enough, just leave because it will never be more or less. No matter what you do, you will never destroy their bad attitudes or create in them more energy to reciprocate the love and attention.

Don't do it!

1. **Communication (Or the lack of)**

   One of the surest signs of a dwindling relationship is a lack of communication. This could range from him ignoring you whenever possible to him just not seeming interested in talking or sharing anything with you. He tries to cut you off and end the conversation, saying he is busy or making excuses not to carry on a chat. It's not only verbal communication; his body language and eye contact may also start seeming disconnected. He seems to be closing himself off, stops sharing anything with you, and seems withdrawn and quiet. Where do you think more energy will come from, and when? Don't stay. Don't do it!

2. **He Can Go Days Without Calling Or Texting**

   They say a gentleman never keeps a lady waiting. But if your man seems to be taking hours and days to reply to a text, call you back, or completely neglect your efforts, there may be a severe issue at hand. There is no consistency in his behaviour and no routine in his communication. He may message you every morning for a few days and then suddenly stop for days on end. This detachment and unresponsiveness could be a sign.

If your man is into you, he will make it a point to reply or call you back as soon as possible. Maybe it's time to realise he's just not that into you! The same can happen with a lady. He will never have more energy to be different. Do not stay. Don't do it!

3. Affection and Intimacy Have Gone 'Poof'

He or she seems irritated by the sweet nothings you whisper into his ear. Those small signs of affection don't seem to exist any longer. Holding hands, a stolen kiss, a hug from behind, looking into each other's eyes, or cuddling—he or she doesn't seem to be in the mood ever. The lack of intimacy from his or her side is a clear sign that something is wrong in the relationship. He or she also seems to be missing birthdays and anniversaries and is not keen to be romantic in any way. If he or she loves you, they know these little things will make you smile and be happy. But if they don't seem to make him or her happy, there's trouble brewing in paradise. That trouble is insufficient energy. Can you create more of it? No! Don't you dare even try.

4. He/she Doesn't Want To Connect

Are you feeling like you're the one making all the efforts? Be it trying to have a conversation or fixing an appointment with a relationship counsellor, you are trying to do everything to salvage this union. But he or she just doesn't seem like they want to. He or she ignores the topics of discussion, walks away, picks fights with you, and makes excuses not to see a counsellor. Let them go. If they don't want to, you can't make them. And you don't want to be in a forced relationship.

Lack of effort, apathy, and avoidance are signs that you should move on; the energy sucks, and there is nothing you can do about it. You cannot create or destroy it.

5. The Words Don't Come Easily To Him

Indeed, love is more than just words, and actions matter too. But if he is not feeling it, he will not say it, no matter how much you hope and try to prod it out of him. I mean, telling you that he loves you. If he is not showing it, chances are he is not in love. There is nothing you can do. Don't do it!

This applies to all aspects of your life. If the energy is not enough, do not try to do anything with it; it will never be. Leave spaces that lack the right energy.

Chapter Forty-Four

The Art of Sorry

If there is one simple life lesson I have learnt, it is to apologise when I am wrong. I had a close friend with whom I shared many life experiences. He stopped talking to me one day and became very cordial. I had no idea what was wrong. When I asked, he kept saying, "Don't act like you don't know what's wrong." After a while, after so much had been destroyed, he said, "You fail to simply say sorry when you are wrong. You always explain and justify your mistakes."

I never explained why I was wrong after that day, but instead apologised and have since had meaningful professional and personal relationships. You, too, can learn to sincerely apologise when you make a mistake.

Try it; you will thank me later.

Chapter Forty-Five

Resource Vs Source

If I happen to fumble here, please pardon me. I have never been to an electrical engineering lecture or class, but I have a bit of understanding. I am this apologetic because I am not so confident in what I am about to say, but I want to succinctly express a thought about understanding the resources we have in life and the sources of success.

Let me use an electrical circuit to get my message across. Let us assume that the socket is the resource that has electricity, and the plug is the source that connects in order to power whatever appliance is performing its function. Maybe let me start by explaining and breaking down the electrical circuit into points that I will use to drive my life lesson about the resources we have in life and how sources need to make use of the resources.

Plugging a plug into a socket completes an electrical circuit, allowing electrical current to flow from the power source to the device or appliance connected to the plug.

The Weight We Carry: A Blueprint for Dealing with Life's Burdens

The plug: The plug is the device that you insert into the socket. It typically has two or three metal prongs, known as pins or blades, which are connected to the wires inside the plug. That is you, as a source, wired to succeed with different or multiple talents.

The socket: The socket is the receptacle or outlet into which you insert the plug. It has corresponding slots or holes that match the configuration of the plug's prongs. This is the resource from which you will gain clarity about your talents, but you need to align with the resource. For instance, you need a mentor whose interests and skills are aligned with what you want to achieve. I will explain this further.

Electrical wiring: Inside the plug, there are wires that are connected to the prongs. These wires carry the electrical current from the power source to the device being powered. The wires are usually colour-coded, with the live wire (also known as the hot wire) typically coloured black or red, the neutral wire coloured white or light grey, and the ground wire coloured green or green with yellow stripes. These are your competing goals and things you want in life: buying a car or building a house, loading data or buying food, etc.

Prong alignment: The plug is inserted into the socket in a specific orientation to ensure proper alignment of the prongs with the corresponding slots in the socket. The prongs are designed to fit securely into the slots and make contact with the conducting parts of the socket. If you find yourself in places that do not match your talents, dreams, background, and plans, you will never fit the resources in that area, and you will miss the power to forge ahead. We often look for energy in the wrong places and with the wrong people.

Contact and connection: When the plug is inserted fully into the socket, the prongs make contact with the conducting parts inside the socket. The live wire of the plug connects to the live terminal in the socket, the neutral wire connects to the neutral terminal, and the ground wire connects to the ground terminal. This completes the electrical circuit. If you align the plug but do not push it in, it will not get power. The same way people have resources but do not go all in to use them, they are like gifted soccer players who undermine going to practice and struggle with fitness. Like a singer who eats anything and everything, not aligning their diet to the demands of their voice.

What am I saying? I am trying to ask you to imagine that our journey through life is like a series of electrical connections. Just as plugging a plug into a socket completes a circuit, allowing electrical current to flow, our achievements and successes are the result of various connections we make along the way.

There are no self-made millionaires, executives, or whatever. We are the sum total of the people we meet, the environments we are exposed to, etc.

The plug represents our own efforts, skills and hard work. It symbolises the energy and dedication we invest in pursuing our goals and dreams. Just like plugging in the plug is essential for electricity to flow, our personal commitment and action are fundamental in driving our progress and accomplishments.

The reason most children from rich families struggle to make it in life is because they grow up with everything at their disposal (resources) and do not make an effort to understand how those are acquired.

Now, let's consider the socket as an external source that contributes to our success. The socket represents the people, opportunities, and resources that support and facilitate our journey. Just as the plug relies on the socket for power, we rely on these external factors to enhance and amplify our efforts.

The socket can include mentors, teachers, and role models who provide guidance and inspiration. They offer valuable insights, share their experiences, and help us develop our skills and talents. They are like the electrical connections that ensure the current flows smoothly, empowering us to achieve our goals.

Additionally, the socket can represent the opportunities we encounter in life. These opportunities may arise unexpectedly, just as a socket awaits the plug. They can come in the form of a chance meeting, a fortunate coincidence, or being at the right place at the right time. Recognising and seizing these opportunities can propel us forward on our path to success.

Furthermore, the socket encompasses the resources and support systems that assist us. It can include financial assistance, access to education or training, a supportive network of family and friends, or even technological advancements that simplify our endeavours. These resources act as conduits, allowing our potential to be fully realised.

By acknowledging and appreciating the role of both the plug (our personal efforts) and the socket (the external sources) in our success, we cultivate a deeper understanding of the interconnectedness of achievement. Just as a plug without a socket remains disconnected, recognising and leveraging the various sources of support in our lives can lead to greater opportunities, growth and fulfillment.

In conclusion, like plugging a plug into a socket to complete an electrical circuit, our success in life stems from the combination of our personal efforts (the plug) and external sources of support (the socket). By recognising and valuing these diverse sources, we can cultivate a stronger foundation for our journey, enabling us to thrive and achieve our fullest potential.

Today's life necessitates a wide range of skills, connections, and a substantial amount of general knowledge. Do not be a plug who just sits there because your kettle won't boil, your television won't turn on, or your cooker won't heat up. Connect yourself to the appropriate sockets in your life and function as intended. The idea that people are self-made is fundamentally flawed, and it has kept many people from achieving success. Go out there and connect to the right platforms, make all the necessary connections, and gather the necessary power or energy.

Chapter Forty-Six

Dare To Use It

Lamarck's most imaginative theory of development, which coined the law of use and disuse, amused me. I must confess that I believe he was merely joking, but there are some important life lessons to be drawn from his unthinkable understanding of human development.

For context, Jean-Baptiste Lamarck, a French biologist, proposed the theory of use and disuse—also referred to as the theory of inheritance of acquired characteristics—in the early 19th century. According to this theory, an organism can change during its lifetime in response to its environment, and these acquired changes can be passed on to its offspring.

Lamarck suggested that when an organism uses a particular organ or structure extensively, it becomes more developed and stronger, while disuse of an organ weakens and diminishes it over time. He believed that these changes would be inherited by the next generation, leading to evolutionary progress.

For example, Lamarck argued that the long neck of a giraffe evolved because ancestral giraffes stretched their necks to reach leaves higher up in trees.

Through continuous stretching and effort, the necks of giraffes became longer, and this acquired characteristic was passed on to subsequent generations.

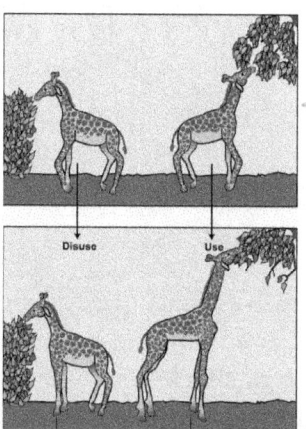

The same way people do not use their talents, the talents just disappear.' But for those who use them, they actually grow better. a garden filled with various plants and flowers. Each plant has unique characteristics and abilities, just like the talents and gifts within individuals. However, for these plants to thrive and reach their full potential, they require care, attention, and utilisation.

When a gardener tends to the garden, watering and nurturing the plants, they flourish and grow. The gardener knows that if they neglect certain plants and withhold water or sunlight, those plants may wither and diminish in vitality over time due to disuse.

Similarly, in life, individuals possess talents and gifts that can be compared to the plants in the garden. If they actively engage and utilise their talents, dedicating time and effort to develop them further, they can grow and flourish.

The Weight We Carry: A Blueprint for Dealing with Life's Burdens

Just as well-nurtured plants produce beautiful blooms and abundant fruits, individuals who use their talents can reap the rewards of their hard work.

On the other hand, if individuals neglect their talents, failing to invest time and effort in honing their skills, their abilities may gradually diminish. Just as plants deprived of water and sunlight become weaker and less vibrant, unused talents may fade and become less impactful over time.

Basically, we ought to be in motion in order to do better in life. It is through the use of our talents, thoughts, etc. that we learn and improve. Effectively, life is like a journey on a train. We all start at different stations with unique destinations in mind. Along the way, we encounter various landscapes, meet different people, and face unexpected challenges.

The train symbolises the passage of time by constantly moving forward. Just as we cannot stop or reverse the train's course, we cannot pause or turn back time in our lives. We must make the most of the journey and embrace the opportunities that come our way.

The different stations represent milestones and transitions in life—birth, education, career choices, relationships, and personal growth. Each station offers a chance for us to reflect, make decisions, and embark on new paths.

The landscapes through which the train passes represent the diversity of experiences in life—joyful moments, scenic beauty, challenging terrains, and even dark tunnels of hardship. These experiences shape us, teach us valuable lessons, and contribute to our personal growth.

The people we meet on the train are like the companions and relationships we encounter in our lives. Some join us for a short duration, while others stay with us for the long haul. They influence us, inspire us, and add richness to our journey.

The challenges we face are akin to obstacles on the train tracks—unexpected delays, detours, or even breakdowns. They test our resilience, problem-solving skills, and determination. Overcoming these challenges makes us stronger and better prepared for the future.

Ultimately, the journey on the train represents the passage of our lives. It reminds us to cherish each moment, learn from our experiences, appreciate the company of others, and navigate through the ups and downs with courage and optimism.

Chapter Forty-Seven

Conspicuous Flexing

Conspicuous flexing, also known as flexing or showing off, refers to the act of ostentatiously displaying one's wealth, possessions, or accomplishments in order to impress others or gain social status. It involves deliberately drawing attention to one's material possessions, achievements, or lifestyle in a way that is intended to provoke envy or admiration from others.

Imagine a peacock in the animal kingdom. Male peacocks have vibrant, colourful feathers that they display in an extravagant manner, spreading their tail feathers to attract attention. Analogously, a person engaging in conspicuous flexing is like a peacock in a social setting. They constantly seek attention and admiration from others by flaunting their material possessions, accomplishments, or lifestyle in a showy and ostentatious way.

Similarly, individuals engaging in conspicuous flexing might gain temporary admiration or attention from others due to their displays of wealth, achievements, or luxurious lifestyle. They may experience a sense of validation and momentarily elevate their social status.

However, just as a peacock's display may be seen as excessive or superficial, individuals who engage in conspicuous flexing may be perceived as shallow or materialistic. The focus on external displays of wealth and status can overshadow their genuine qualities and character. It can strain authentic relationships, as others may question their motives or see through the façade. Additionally, the pressure to maintain the image of wealth and success can lead to financial strain, debt, and dissatisfaction when the desired level of validation is not achieved.

Conspicuous flexing is often associated with the desire for social validation and the need to project an image of success. It can manifest in various forms, such as flaunting expensive cars, designer clothing, luxury vacations, or displaying lavish homes. In the age of social media, conspicuous flexing has become more prevalent, with individuals sharing carefully curated images and stories to present an idealised version of their lives.

These are the most notable signs of someone bogging down under the pressures of life, rich or poor:

1. **Social validation:** Conspicuous flexing often stems from a desire for social validation and recognition. Individuals may seek approval and admiration from others, using their possessions or accomplishments as a means to gain status and acceptance within their social circles.

2. **Insecurity and self-esteem:** Some individuals may engage in conspicuous flexing as a way to compensate for personal insecurities or low self-esteem. By showcasing their material wealth or achievements, they may hope to bolster their self-worth and feel more confident.

3. **Societal pressure:** Society, particularly in certain cultures or subcultures, can place significant importance on material possessions and outward displays of success. The pressure to conform to societal standards of wealth and status can drive individuals to engage in conspicuous flexing as a means of fitting in or standing out.

When I was writing this chapter, I had seen over ten posts in a day in which people showed how much their clothes were worth, what cars they drove, and where they ate. In most of these cases, I've discovered that these people do not like the person they see in the mirror when no one else is watching. Their fridges are mostly empty, just like most apartment dwellers in Midrand who do not have furniture. This is because keeping up appearances can come at a significant cost. Individuals who engage in conspicuous flexing may face financial pressure as they attempt to maintain a lifestyle that exceeds their means. This can lead to excessive debt, financial stress, and an inability to sustain the extravagant image they seek to project.

The pressure to constantly prove oneself can lead to chronic stress and burnout. The constant striving, high expectations, and self-imposed pressure can take a toll on one's mental and physical well-being. It can lead to exhaustion, anxiety, and a decreased ability to enjoy life outside of the pursuit of validation.

I know it took me long to say this, but people don't care after scrolling down their timelines.

Chapter Forty-Eight

Life Balance Sheet

What is your accounting equation?

Equity= Assets - Liabilities or Liabilities = Assets - Equity

The summary of differences between them are given below:

BASIS OF DIFFERENCE	EQUITY	LIABILITIES
Definition	It is the money invested by owners in the business	It is the money owed by the company
Purpose	Used for buying assets or discharging debts of company	Liabilities are burden to the company and are paid off by the company in due course
Classification	Divided into equity share capital, preference share capital, reserves and surplus etc.	Classified as current and non-current liabilities
Ownership	Equity is the fund of owner	Funds go out from the company in payment of liabilities
Accounting equation	Equity = Assets - Liabilities	Liabilities = Assets - Equity

Nature	Equity is the source of funds to acquire resources	Liabilities arise during procurement of funds and application of funds.
Link with income statement	Retained earnings link equity with income statement.	There is no direct link between liabilities and income statement
Line items	Equity consists of contributed capital, treasury stock, preferred shares and retained earnings.	The line items consist of notes payable, long term debts, advance receipts, accounts payables, etc.

Equity represents the ownership interest in a company, assets represent the resources owned by the company; and liabilities represent the company's obligations to creditors.

These three elements together make up the basic accounting equation: Assets = Liabilities + Equity.

Meet Raisibe and Raesetša. They value three main aspects of their lives: career, personal growth and social relationships.

Raisibe and Raesetša's careers are important to them, as they find fulfilment and satisfaction through their work. They also prioritise personal growth by pursuing learning opportunities, acquiring new skills, and expanding their knowledge. Additionally, Raisibe and Raesetša value their social relationships and believe in maintaining strong connections with friends and loved ones.

However, Raisibe and Raesetša face various liabilities in their lives. They have demanding work responsibilities that often require long hours and dedication. They also have personal goals and aspirations that require time and effort to pursue.

Additionally, Raisibe and Raesetša need to allocate time and energy to nurture their social relationships.

To achieve equity, Raisibe and Raesetša make conscious choices to balance their priorities. They set boundaries at work to maintain a healthy work-life balance, ensuring they have time for personal growth and social connections. Raisibe and Raesetša may dedicate certain evenings or weekends solely for personal development activities like attending workshops or taking online courses. They also make an effort to plan regular social outings and gatherings to strengthen their relationships.

Raisibe and Raesetša understand that a perfect balance may not always be possible as priorities and circumstances change. In busier work periods, they may need to allocate more time to their career, while in quieter periods, they may dedicate extra time to personal growth or socialising. Raisibe and Raesetša communicate their needs and priorities to their colleagues, friends, and loved ones to manage expectations and foster understanding.

By regularly reassessing their priorities and making intentional choices, Raisibe and Raesetša strive to achieve equity in their lives. They aim to find a balance that allows them to excel in their career, pursue personal growth, and cultivate meaningful social relationships.

They understand that different areas of life may have competing demands, making it challenging to allocate resources and make decisions. For example, you might face a conflict between spending time with family and pursuing career opportunities. It requires careful evaluation and prioritisation to navigate these conflicts effectively.

The Weight We Carry: A Blueprint for Dealing with Life's Burdens

When you prioritise certain aspects of your life, you may feel guilty about not giving enough attention to others. Sacrifices might need to be made, and it can be emotionally challenging to let go of certain commitments or opportunities. Balancing conflicting priorities often involves trade-offs and finding a sense of acceptance.

How does your life balance sheet look? Do you have more liabilities, such as a preference for going out every weekend over your work and plans? Do you find it difficult to spend quality time with your family because you have too much work to do and are always behind schedule? It means that your liabilities far outnumber your assets. Do you drive a car that breaks down every month and forces you to borrow money from friends and family to make ends meet? You are on the verge of depression. If you feel stressed in any aspect of your life, go back and check every single item on your life balance sheet and correct any imbalances.

Chapter Forty-Nine

Body, Mind and Money

On October 19, 2022, I met a notable scholar in the field of indigenous knowledge and commercialisation. The meeting was supposed to be between a driver and an invited guest at the 2nd African Traditional and Natural Product Medicine Conference, but the unexpected happened.

Dr Moses who was based in the United Kingdom at the time and served in the British Monarchy under King Charles III, doctored not only indigenous knowledge systems but also organic success factors.

As we rushed to the Conference's welcome gala dinner after meeting him at the Polokwane International Airport around 17h30, he told myself and Lebogang Mokaze, with whom we met Dr Moses, that he was a fan of the kasi lifestyle. He would rather take a taxi from the airport to The Ranch Resort, where the conference was held.

He told us that our network is our net worth and that there is a potential rich scheme in our circle that we could establish through group savings, commonly known as stokvel.

But, in the process, he stated that three factors determine our fate: body, mind, and soul.

Body, mind, and money are interconnected aspects of our lives that can greatly influence each other. Let's explore how they work together:

Body and Mind:

The body and mind are closely intertwined, and their well-being impacts each other. Taking care of your physical health through regular exercise, proper nutrition, and sufficient rest can enhance your mental well-being. Physical activity releases endorphins, which can improve your mood and reduce stress. Similarly, maintaining good mental health through practices like meditation, mindfulness, and engaging in activities you enjoy can positively impact your physical well-being.

Mind and Money:

The state of your mind can significantly influence your financial situation. Your mindset, attitudes, and beliefs about money can shape your financial decisions and behaviours. A positive mindset with regards to money can lead to prudent financial choices, such as saving, investing, and seeking opportunities for growth. Conversely, negative thought patterns or impulsive behaviour may lead to poor financial outcomes, such as excessive spending, debt, or missed opportunities.

Moreover, having mental clarity, focus, and resilience can positively impact your professional life, opening doors for career advancement, promotions, and increased income.

Body and Money:

The relationship between the body and money is multifaceted. On the one hand, your physical well-being can impact your financial situation. Poor health can result in medical expenses, reduced productivity, and missed work opportunities, potentially affecting your income and financial stability. Furthermore, maintaining good physical health can lead to increased energy levels, productivity, and job performance, potentially opening avenues for financial growth.

On the other hand, your financial status can influence your ability to take care of your body. Access to quality healthcare, nutritious food, fitness facilities, and other wellness resources often requires financial resources. Having financial stability can provide the means to invest in your physical well-being through healthcare, fitness programmes, and a balanced lifestyle.

He asked me to imagine a three-legged stool. Each leg represents one aspect: body, mind, and money. For the stool to be stable and functional, all three legs need to be strong and balanced.

The leg representing the body represents your physical health and well-being. It's like the foundation of the stool. If this leg is weak or neglected, the stool becomes wobbly and unstable. Taking care of your body through exercise, proper nutrition, and rest is essential for maintaining stability.

The Weight We Carry: A Blueprint for Dealing with Life's Burdens

The leg representing the mind represents your mental health and mindset. It's like the seat of the stool, where you find balance and support. If this leg is weakened by negative thoughts, stress, or a lack of clarity, the stool becomes uncomfortable and difficult to sit on. Nurturing your mind through mindfulness, positive thinking, and self-care is vital for finding balance and stability.

The leg representing money represents your financial well-being. It's like the third leg that completes the stool. If this leg is weak or unbalanced, the stool becomes lopsided and unreliable. Managing your finances wisely, having a positive relationship with money, and making sound financial decisions contribute to the stability and security of the stool.

Just as a stool with one weak or imbalanced leg cannot provide proper support, neglecting any of these aspects in your life can lead to imbalance and dissatisfaction. By strengthening and maintaining all three legs of the stool—body, mind, and money—you can create a solid foundation for a well-rounded and fulfilling life.

Chapter Fifty

Epilogue

Dear Reader,

As I sit here, okay on the banks of the Ebenezer Dam, penning these final words, I can't help but feel a mix of emotions—gratitude, nostalgia and a tinge of melancholy. This journey we've been on together has been nothing short of remarkable. The experiences we've shared, the lessons we've learned, and the growth we've undergone have transformed us in ways we couldn't have imagined.

Looking back to the nurturing days of my childhood, I see the seeds of curiosity and wonder that were sown, which blossomed into a thirst for knowledge and a passion for exploration. Those early years set the stage for the person I would become, and I am forever indebted to the love and care that shaped my foundation.

Growing up, life threw countless challenges my way—some anticipated, others unexpected. I stumbled and fell, but I also picked myself up time and time again. In those moments of struggle, I discovered the tenacity within me and the resilience that would carry me through the toughest of times.

The Weight We Carry: A Blueprint for Dealing with Life's Burdens

Decisions—big and small—became the building blocks of my destiny. It wasn't always easy to know which path to take, but with each choice, I learned to trust my intuition and embrace the consequences, whether they led to triumph or introspection. I learned that even when uncertainty and fear knocked on my door, I had the strength to face them head-on.

The pressures of society tried to mould me into something I wasn't, but I found the courage to break free from those chains and embrace my authentic self. It was liberating to shed the weight of expectations and walk the path that felt right for me, even if it diverged from the norm.

Throughout this journey, I've navigated the complexities of relationships—professional, personal, romantic, family, and social. I've made mistakes, but I've also experienced the beauty of forgiveness and the power of genuine connection. These relationships have been the pillars that supported me during life's storms and the celebrations that filled my heart with joy.

Financial matters were once an enigma, but I realised that financial literacy and investment were key to securing my future. I learned to manage my resources wisely and to appreciate the value of financial security without letting it overshadow the pursuit of true fulfilment.

Mental health emerged as a vital aspect of my well-being. I confronted the stigma surrounding mental health head-on, seeking help and support when needed. Embracing vulnerability became a gateway to strength, and self-care became a non-negotiable part of my routine.

As I conclude this book, I understand that life's journey is an ever-evolving one. It's not about reaching a specific destination but about savouring each step of the way.

I've come to realise that the beauty of life lies not in its predictability but in its unpredictability—a blank canvas on which I can paint my dreams and aspirations.

So, dear reader, as we part ways, I leave you with this: Embrace life with open arms. Cherish the moments of joy, persevere through the challenges, and savour the triumphs. Trust your instincts, be kind to yourself, and follow the compass of your heart. Know that it's okay to stumble, for it is through those moments that we grow stronger.

Thank you for being a part of this journey with me. Our paths may diverge, but the memories we've shared will forever remain etched in my heart. Here's to new beginnings, to embracing uncertainty, and to living a life that is authentically ours.

The weight you carry is the same weight every black child carries. Your offspring will help you carry it and inherit the burden, should you not take this time and chance to put it down and start afresh.

With love and gratitude,

Moses Moreroa

Bibliography

Arvey, R. D., Dewhirst, H. D., & Boling, J. C. (1976). Relationships between goal clarity, participation in goal setting, and personality characteristics on job satisfaction in a scientific organization. *Journal of Applied Psychology*, 61(1), 103-105.

Bressler, M., Bressler, L., & Bressler, M. (2010). The role and relationship of hope, optimism and goal setting in academic success: A study of students enrolled in online accounting courses. *Academy of Educational Leadership Journal*, 14, 37-51.

Cott, C., & Finch, E. (1991). Goal-setting in physical therapy practice. *Physiotherapy Canada*, 43, 19-22.

Davidai, S. and Gilovich, T. (2018). The ideal road not taken: The self-discrepancies involved in people's most enduring regrets. *Emotion*, 18(3): 439–452.

Erez, M. (1977). Feedback: A necessary condition for the goal setting-performance relationship. *Journal of Applied Psychology*, 62, 624-627.

Hattie, J., & Timperley, H. (2007). The power of feedback. Review of Educational Research, 77, 81-112.

Hertiz-Lazarowitz, R., Kirdus, V. B., & Miller, N. (1992). *Implications of current research on cooperative interaction for classroom application.* In R. Hertz-Lazarowtiz & N. Miller (Eds.). Interaction in cooperative groups: The theoretical anatomy of group learning. New York, NY: Cambridge University Press.

Holliday, R. C., Ballinger, C., & Playford, E.D. (2007). Goal setting in neurological rehabilitation: Patients' perspectives, disability and rehabilitation. *Reader in Occupational Therapy*, 29, 389-394.

Ivancevich, J. M., & McMahon, J. T. (1982). The effects of goal setting, external feedback, and self-generated feedback on outcome variables: A field experiment. *Academy of Management Journal*, 25(2), 359-372.

Kaiser, P., Tullar, W., & McKowen, D. (2000). Student team projects by internet. *Business Communication Quarterly*, 63, 75-82.

Klein, H. J., Austin, J. T., & Cooper, J. T. (2008). *Goal choices and decision processes*. In R. Kanfer, G. Chen, & R. D. Pritchard (Eds). Work motivation: Past, present, and future. New York, NY: Routledge.

Kleinginna, P., & Kleinginna, A. (1981). A categorized list of motivation definitions, with suggestions for a consensual definition. *Motivation and Emotion*, 5, 263-291.

Kristof-Brown, A. L., & Stevens, C. K. (2001). Goal congruence in project teams: Does the fit between members' personal mastery and performance goals matter? *Journal of Applied Psychology*, 86(6), 1083-1095.

Latham, G. P. (2004). The motivational benefits of goal setting. *Management Perspectives*, 18, (4), 126—129.

Latham, G. P., & Locke, E. A. (1979). Goal setting: A motivational technique that works. *Organizational Dynamics*, 8, 68-80.

Latham, G. P., & Locke, E. A. (2006). Enhancing the benefits and overcoming the pitfalls of goal setting. *Organizational Dynamics*, 35, 332-340.

Locke, E. (2019). Edwin Locke on are you setting effective goals? Podcast with Professor Edwin Locke. [Audio podcast] Retrieved from https://www.michellemcquaid.com/podcast/mppw44-edwin-locke/

Locke, E. A. & Latham, G. P. (2013). *New developments in goal setting and task performance.* New York, NY: Routledge.

Locke, E. A. (1996). Motivation through conscious goal setting. *Applied & Preventive Psychology,* 5, 117-124.

Locke, E. A. (2001). *Motivation by goal setting.* In R. T. Golembiewski (Ed). Handbook of organizational behavior, second edition, revised and expanded. New York, NY: Marcel Dekker.

Locke, E. A., & Latham, G. P. (1990). *A theory of goal setting & task performance.* Englewood Cliffs, NJ: Prentice-Hall.

Locke, E. A., & Latham, G. P. (2002). Building a practically useful theory of goal setting and task motivation: A 35-year odyssey, *American Psychologist,* 57, 705–717.

Locke, E. A., Smith, K. G., Erez, M. E., Chah, D. O., & Shaffer, A. (1994). The effects of intra-individual goal conflict on performance. *Journal of Management,* 20, 67-91.

Macan, T. H., Shahani, C., Dipboye, R. L., & Phillips, A. P. (1990). College students' time management: Correlations with academic performance and stress. *Journal of Educational Psychology,* 82(4), 760-768.

MacLeod, A. K., Coates, E., & Hetherton, J. (2008). Increasing well-being through teaching goal-setting and planning skills: Results of a brief intervention. *Journal of Happiness Studies,* 9(2), 185-196.

Martin, G., & Pear, J. P. (2019). *Behavior modification: What it is and how to do it (11th ed.).* New York, NY: Routledge.

Mayer, J. D. (2004). What is emotional intelligence? UNH Personality Lab. Retrieved from https://scholars.unh.edu/personality_lab/8

McCoach, D. B., & Siegle, D. (2003). The School Attitude Assessment Survey-Revised: A new instrument to identify academically able students who underachieve. *Educational and Psychological Measurement*, 63, 414-429.

McCurdy, M., Skinner, C. H., Grantham, K., Watson, T. S., & Hindman, P. M. (2001). Increasing on-task behavior in an elementary student during mathematics seatwork by interspersing additional brief problems. *School Psychology Review*, 30, 23- 32.

Mind Statistics. (n.d.). Money & mental health. Retrieved from https://www.mind.org.uk/information-support/tips-for-everyday-living/money-and-mental-health/#.XH-UZfn7TIV

Miner, J. B. (2005). *Organizational behaviour 1: Essential theories of motivation and leadership*. Oxon, UK: Routledge.

Morisano, D., Hirsh, J. B., Peterson, J. B., Pihl, R. O., & Shore, B. M. (2010). Setting, elaborating, and reflecting on personal goals improves academic performance. *Journal of Applied Psychology*, 95(2), 255-264.

Naka, M., & Naoi, H. (1995). The effect of repeated writing on memory. *Memory and Cognition*, 23, 201-212.

Powell, A., Piccoli, G., & Ives, B. (2004). Virtual teams: a review of current literature and directions for future research. *ACM SIGMIS Database: The DATABASE for Advances in Information Systems*, 35(1), 6-36.

Reis, S. M., & McCoach, D. B. (2000). The underachievement of gifted students: What do we know and where do we go? *Gifted Child Quarterly*, 44, 152-170

Rose, G., & Smith, L. (2018). Mental health recovery, goal setting and working alliance in an Australian community-managed organisation. *Health Psychology Open*, 5(1), 1-9.

Ryan, T. A. (1970). *Intentional behavior*. New York, NY: Ronald Press.

Schunk, D. H. (1985). Participation in goal setting: Effects on self-efficacy and skills of learning-disabled children. *The Journal of Special Education*, 19(3), 307–317.

Seijts, G. H., & Latham, G. P. (2000). The effects of goal setting and group size on performance in a social dilemma. *Canadian Journal of Behavioural Science*, 32, 104–116

Smith, K., Locke, E., & Barry, D. (1990). Goal setting, planning, and organizational performance: An experimental simulation. *Organizational Behavior and Human Decision Processes*, 46, 118-134.

Thomas, G. and Husted, V. (1994). The temporal pattern to the experience of regret. *Journal of Personality and Social Psychology*, 67(3): 357-365.

Vincent, P. J., Boddana, P., & MacLeod, A. K. (2004). Positive life goals and plans in parasuicide. *Clinical Psychology & Psychotherapy: An International Journal of Theory & Practice*, 11(2), 90-99.

Zimmerman, B. J. (2008). *Goal setting: A key proactive source of academic self-regulation*. In D. H. Shunk & B. J. Zimmerman (Eds). Motivation and self-regulated learning: Theory, research, and applications. Abingdon, UK: Taylor & Francis.

Zimmerman, B. J., Bandura, A., & Martinez-Pons, M. (1992). Self-motivation for academic attainment: The role of self-efficacy beliefs and personal goal setting. *American Educational Research Journal*, 29(3), 663-676.

Index

2

2nd African Traditional and Natural Product Medicine Conference, 258

A

À Rebours, 55
Africa, 2, 3, 26, 28, 61, 63, 152, 153
Akan culture, 204
Alain de Botton, 55
aloe vera, 58
American Psychological Association, **xv**, **xvi**
Americans, 217
Anna Sorokin, 102
Anticipation, 47, 49, 52, 53
Apple, 39
Arnold Schwarzenegger, 176
Arthur Masoma, 47
Australia, 36

B

Baskin Robbins, 45
Bible, 45, 89, 109, 164, 166, 192
Bill Bowerman, 60
Black Tax, 194, 195, 196
Bonang Lite, 218
Brene Brown, 135
British Monarchy, 258
Broadway, 129
Bryanston, 47

BusinessTech, 153

C

CAF Champions League, 39
Cardiff, 27
Carly Simon, 49, 52
Catch-22, 120, 159
Charles Cooley, 214
Charles Dickens, 56
Charlie Munger, 161
Chinese, 27
Chris Excel, 218
Christian, 173
Christmas, 53
Cognitive Behavioural Therapy, **xv**
Corinthians, **ix**
COVID-19, 61

D

Daring Greatly, 135
Day of the Week Moods, 50
Debengeni Falls, 171
Delilah, 164
Denzel Washington, 127, 128
Des Esseintes, 56
Dezry Kay, 47
digital detox, 98, 137, 220
DJ, 218
Dopamine, 96
Dr Moses, 258
Drakensberg, 143

Dubai, 58
Duc des Esseintes, 55
Dutch, 55

E

Ebenezer Dam, 262
Elizabeth Holmes, 101
eNeuro, 55
English, 56, 176
Estonia, 20
Europe, 26

F

Fabiani, 155
Fences, 129
Finland, 20
FOMO, 218
Fundi, 30

G

GaMamabolo, 143, 221
GaMothapo, 201
Gauteng Province, 3
Gaza, 164
Ghana, 204
Global South, 33
glossophobia, 132
God, 50, 164, 165, 166
Goliath, 16
Gospel of Matthew, 189
GPS, 47, 48

H

Haenertsburg, 3, 143
Harry Potter, 130
Hartley, 54
Harvard, 26, 137
Hasta la vista, 176
Hawaii, 45
Herbalife, 147
Houtbosdorp, 169
Hwiti, 143

I

Industrial Revolution, 33
Information Giants (Pty) Ltd, 3
Information Giants Publishers™, 3, v
Instagram, 22, 95, 96, 217
Instagram,, 95, 96
iPad, 99
iPhone, 34

J

J.K. Huysman, 55
J.K. Rowling, 130
J.M. Barrie, 212
Janet Polivy, 31
Jean-Baptiste Lamarck, 247
Judges, 164, 165

K

Khalo, 94
King Charles III, 258
Kromdraai Blomme, 170

L

Lamarck, 247
Latvia, 20
Lebogang, 90, 234, 235, 258
Lebogang Mokaze, 90, 258
Lebowa Government, 169
Lerato "LKG" Kganyago, 218
Lethabo Hlahla, 171
Liberty Institute of Strategic Marketing, 153
Limpopo, 26, 63, 67, 147, 201
Lithuania, 20

M

Makgopheng, 221
Makhadzi, 114
Malehufa, 183, 184
Markham's, 155
Matome, 143, 144
Mazama, 198, 199
Mental health, xi, xii, xiv, 219, 263, 269
mianzi, 27
Michael, 201, 202
Midrand, 3, 253
Mohlokomedi, 221, 222
Molly, 20
Molotov cocktail, 19, 20, 21, 22, 23, 24, 25
Molotov-Ribbentrop Pact, 20
Monare, 169
Monday blues, 48, 49
Moremogolo, 94
Moreroa, 3, 155, 264
Moses Moreroa, vi
Mosima, 201, 202
Motlanalo, 170
Motume, 169, 170, 171
Mphogodiba, 169
Mullainathan, 26

N

Nazi Germany, 20
Netflix, 46
New York, 102, 139, 265, 266, 267, 268, 269
Nike, 60
Nordic countries, 33
NSFAS, 30
Nthabiseng, 147

O

Old Testament, 197
Orlando Pirates, 223

P

Pablo Picasso, 64
Panado, 94
Paris, 56
Pat Williams, 91
Paul, 44, 47, 200, 202
Pedi, 47
Peter, 31, 68, 200, 202, 212, 213
Peter Drucker, 68
Peter Herman, 31
Peter Pan Complex, 212
Peter Pan Syndrome, 212, 213
Philippians, 44, 45
Philistine, 164
Philistines, 165, 167

Pitso Mosimane, 223
placebo effect, 94, 96
Poland, 20
Polokwane, 2, 234, 258
President Obama, 45
Proverbs, 197
Putla 'Nogane', v

R

Raesetša, 256, 257
Rafa Nadal, 54
Raisibe, 256, 257
RDP, 159
Reed Hastings, 46
Relational Paradox, 136
Research, 29, 51, 70, 137, 219, 265, 270
Ricky Rick, 176
Ronald Wayne, 39
Ruth Soukup, 139
Ruud Krol, 223

S

SADAG, 18
Samson, 164, 165, 166, 167
Samsung, 30
San Diego, 103
Sankofa, 204, 205
Science, 130, 135, 269
Sean Covey, 22
Segwashi, 143, 169
Sequoia, 40
Shimon Hayut, 102
Simon Sinek, 60
Snapchat, 95, 96

social media, 19, 21, 71, 95, 96, 97, 98, 118, 134, 137, 216, 217, 218, 219, 220, 252
South Africa, 28
South African, 18, 27, 35
South Wales, 27
Soviet, 20
Spitzkop, 169
Steve Jobs, 39
Steve Wozniak, 39, 40
Success Comes in Seven Pieces, 134

T

TED Talk, 132
Terminator 2, 176
TGIF, 50
Thabo Madisha, 147
Thank God It's Friday, 50
The Art of Travel, 55
The Ranch Resort, 258
The Sunday Night Blues, 50
Thomas Edison, 127, 129
TikTok, 73, 95, 134
Tinder Swindler, 102
Tlou, 54
Truworths, 155
Tshware village, 194
TVET, 33
Twitter, 98, 218

U

UEFA Champions League, 39
UEFA Europa League, 39
Uncle Waffles, 217
University of California, 103

University of Cape Town, **153**
University of Limpopo, 61
University of Pennsylvania, **129**
Uri Gneezy, **103**

V

Valley of Sorek, **164**
Vanessa Van Edwards, **136**
Veekraal, **169**
Victor Kgomoeswana, **147**
VIP, **159**, **218**
Vyacheslav Molotov, **20**

W

Waterfall Business Park, **3**
WhatsApp, **50**, **54**, **216**
Wizit card, **30**

Y

Yale University, **103**
YouTube, **134**

Z

Zoë Chance, **103**

www.ingramcontent.com/pod-product-compliance
Lightning Source LLC
Chambersburg PA
CBHW070137100426
42743CB00013B/2740